PURITY OR POLLUTION

Publishers of the International Library

LIBRAIRIE ERNEST FLAMMARION—France
VERLAG J. F. SCHREIBER—Germany
(in association with Union Verlag, Stuttgart, and Oster, Bundesverlag, Vienna)
WM. COLLINS SONS & CO. LTD.—Great Britain
RIZZOLI EDITORE—Italy
FRANKLIN WATTS, INC.—United States of America

International Consultants

JEAN-FRANÇOIS POUPINEL—France
Ancien Elève Ecole Polytechnique
KLAUS DODERER—Germany
Professor, Frankfurt
MARGARET MEEK—Great Britain
Lecturer, Division of Language Teaching, Institute
of Education, University of London
FAUSTO MARIA BONGIOANNI—Italy
Professor of Education
at the University of Genoa
MARY V. GAVER—United States of America
Professor, Graduate School of Library Science,
Rutgers University

International Editorial Board

HENRI NOGUÈRES
GERHARD SCHREIBER
JAN COLLINS
GIANNI FERRAUTO
HOWARD GRAHAM

INTERNATIONAL LIBRARY

PIERRE RONDIÈRE

PURITY OR POLLUTION

The Struggle for Water

COLLINS · PUBLISHERS
London · Glasgow

FRANKLIN WATTS, INC.
New York

First Edition 1971

ISBN 0 00 100128 0 (*Collins*)
SBN 531 02103 3 (*Franklin Watts*)

ACKNOWLEDGMENTS

Cover: J. Nestgen, Le lac Léman.

Endpapers: Duchêne, P. Rondière.

Drawings and Photographs: Yves Raynaud, *Power* (June 1966), ORSANCO and Irrigation Districts Association of California.

Photos: pp. 6: J. Nestgen. 8: P. Rondière. 9 (top): Duchêne. 9 (bottom): J. Nestgen. 10: OMS/M. Jacot. 11 (top): J. Nestgen. 11 (bottom): Dan Dubert. 15 (top): Joëlle Robert. 15 (bottom): Flammarion. 16 (top): J. Nestgen. 16 (centre): Dan Dubert. 16 (bottom): M. Otthoffer. 17 (top): Flammarion. 17 (bottom): UNESCO/ D. Roger. 18 (top): M. Otthoffer. 18 (bottom): J. Nestgen. 19 (top): AFIP. 19 (bottom): M. Otthoffer. 20: P. Rondière. 21 (top): Yan. 21 (bottom): Roger Perrin. 22 (top): Philippe Claret. 22 (bottom): P. Rondière. 23: Philippe Claret. 24 (top): Flammarion. 24 (bottom): Conservatoire national des Arts et Métiers. 25 (top): Roger Perrin. 25 (bottom): Giraudon. 26: Dan Dubert. 27 (top): Duchêne. 27 (bottom): M. Otthoffer. 28: J. Nestgen. 30 (bottom): Christiane Barrier. 31 (top): J. Nestgen-Y. Raynaud. 31 (bottom): J. Nestgen. 33 (top): Quervain et Le Coq. 33 (bottom): Jacana/M. C. Noailles. 34: Yan. 35: Flammarion. 36: Jean-Louis Moulin. 37: Duchêne. 38: AFIP. 41 (centre): Jacana/Noailles. 42: J. Nestgen. 43 (top): J. Nestgen. 43 (bottom): AFIP. 44 (top): Roger Perrin. 44 (bottom): Yan. 45 (top): Roger Perrin. 45 (bottom): Dan Dubert. 46 (top): Libre-service Actualités. 46 (bottom): Usis. 47: Yan. 48 (top): P. Rondière. 48 (bottom): Jean-Louis Moulin. 49: J. Nestgen. 50: Dan Dubert. 52 (top): Usis. 52 (centre): M. Otthoffer. 52 (bottom): IPS/Usis. 53 (top): J. Nestgen. 53 (bottom): Gérard Tavernier. 54: J. Nestgen. 55 (centre): P. Rondière. 55 (top): J. Nestgen. 55 (bottom): Jean-Louis Moulin. 56 (top): AFIP. 56 (bottom): Roger Perrin. 57: IPS/Usis. 58, 59, 60, 61, 62 and 63: P. Rondière. 65: Dan Dubert. 66: M. Otthoffer. 68: J. Nestgen. 69 (top): J. Nestgen. 69 (bottom): D. Franconin. 70: M. Otthoffer. 71: J. Nestgen. 73 (top): Rapho/ Doisneau. 73 (bottom): Yan. 75: Rapho-Lang Cipha. 76: M. Otthoffer. 79 (top): Yan. 79 (bottom): Amstrong-Rapho. 80 (left): Rapho-Doisneau. 80 (right): UNESCO/ Bibal. 81 (left): M. Boulay. 81 (right): OMS/M. Jacot. 81 (bottom): Dan Dubert. 83 (top): Duchêne. 83 (bottom): AFIP. 84, 85, 86: P. Rondière. 87 (top): UNESCO/ F. Bibal. 87 (bottom): Usis. 89: Usis. 92, 93, 94, 95 (top): Christiane Barrier/Station d'épuration des eaux du Syndicat intercommunal de la région de Corbeil-Essonnes. 98: M. Otthoffer. 100: M. Otthoffer. 101 (top): Joëlle Robert. 101 (bottom): Gérard Tavernier. 103, 105 (top and centre): P. Rondière. 105 (bottom): Jean-Louis Moulin. 106, 107, 108, 109: P. Rondière. 110: J. Nestgen. 112: Dan Dubert. 113 (top): Dan Dubert. 113 (bottom): P. Rondière. 115: P. Rondière. 116 (top): Roger Perrin. 116 (bottom): AFIP. 117: Yan. 118 (top): J. Nestgen. 118 (bottom): P. Rondière. 119: P. Rondière. 121: Carbonnier. 122 (top): J. Nestgen. 122 (bottom): P. Rondière. 123: Duchêne. 125: Patrick Scalbert.

Printed and bound in Great Britain by Jarrold & Sons Ltd, Norwich
Library of Congress Catalog Card Number: 74-153828

CONTENTS

INTRODUCTION

A DAY WITH THE WORLD'S WATER

NEW YORK · In a Fifth Avenue hotel one is intrigued by the presence of a third tap. What is it that they are offering me in addition to the normal hot and cold water? The answer is simply *pure* iced water—water which is palatable, aerated, odourless and reliable. New York knows that its water supply is treated in order to make it safe to drink, and that its taste can be unpleasant in a tooth-glass or can spoil the flavour of whisky. This untainted water is therefore regarded as a luxury. Today's luxury or tomorrow's necessity?

MOSCOW · Caviare is scarce. It is impossible to obtain it in restaurants and it can only be bought in shops specially reserved for foreign tourists. A series of dams on the Volga which control the flow and harness its energy prevent the sturgeons from coming up the river to lay their eggs and hence from breeding. The level of the Caspian Sea is falling, and the fish are disappearing. Is this process irreversible?

PARIS · Below the Pont de l'Alma, his back to the Grand Palais, a few hundred yards from the Champs Elysées, an angler dreamily watches his float. With dangling legs and inattentive eye he lets himself be lulled to sleep by the gently flowing water. He knows that the Seine is so polluted that his chances of a bite are slim indeed. He is really there for the pleasure of relaxing beside the passing river. Can we hope that the fish will return?

LONDON · The peers in the House of Lords no longer fish for salmon between sittings, as they did two centuries ago; they are otherwise preoccupied. If London is not to suffer from shortage of water a few years hence, it might be necessary to construct a huge underground reservoir. Is this feasible?

RIO DE JANEIRO · Refugees from the drought area 200 miles to the north present themselves at the gates of the city, as they have done every morning for the past month, forced to take the road by an abnormal shortage of water. In the *favellas*, the densely populated quarters clinging to the slopes of the granite hills, this is the time when women and children begin their comings and goings, descending to the collecting point at the bottom of the slope to get a few gallons of water and climbing back with their jugs on their heads.

FLORENCE · Students from all over the world swell the ranks of the

Picturesque surroundings at Paray-le-Monial are reflected in the quiet water

The Seine in Paris

The river-bank beside the Kremlin in Moscow

Cairo: the Nile in spate

permanent team which has spent long months restoring the rare books damaged in the disastrous flooding of the Arno, which also inundated and ravaged the town itself. The disappearance of former forests, unchecked soil erosion and the absence of dams for controlling the flow provide the reason for this catastrophe, the worst which the city has experienced and one which threatened and devastated one of the marvels of the world in which we live.

RAS GHAREB · On this part of the Red Sea coast the tide laps gently, its limit marked on the sands by a silky line of foam. Not a tree, not a field, not a chimney or a factory roof breaks the monotony of the landscape. Yet the soil is rich; the nearby range of hills contains deposits of iron and bauxite, and the subsoil yields petroleum. Only one thing is missing which would allow the growth of orange and palm trees and the building of smelting plants, refineries and towns: that thing is water. The brownish water which is drunk here comes every fortnight in a cargo loaded at Suez, together with vegetables, planks and nails, paper and ink, clothing and fruit, meat and matches. Should a desalination plant for sea water be built, or should the subsoil be explored for fresh water?

WASHINGTON · By order of the President of the United States the engineer corps of the American army is carrying out a programme aimed at reducing pollution of the Great Lakes on the northern frontier. Twelve million tons of industrial and domestic waste is discharged annually into this giant complex which lies astride the United States-Canadian border.

Lake Erie, 240 miles long, is in the worst state, but Lake Superior, Lake Ontario . . . all are contaminated, and six resorts have been closed.

KUZNETSK · This basin in southern Siberia contains the richest coal deposits on earth: seams of 45, 60, 90 feet. Why go to the trouble of sinking mines and cutting galleries? Today and every day a water-cannon is brought into play, worked by a single operator. The powerful jet, which could pulverize a man at 50 yards, breaks up, tears out, and washes away the 30 or 36

Living afloat, in crowded conditions, at Hong Kong

Venice at twilight. No town ever grew up far from water, and Venice is a city of water-ways

feet of surface soil. Then bulldozers dig out the coal which has been laid bare and mechanical shovels load it on to wagons.

NEAR FRANKFURT IN GERMANY · A farmer fixes an automatic sprayer to his tractor. To the water which will spray an acre he adds less than half an ounce of a special herbicide. Now nothing will grow there for a whole year but maize. Any other kind of vegetation will be killed.

At the same moment the sun is setting over PETROLINDA ON THE BANKS OF THE SÃO FRANCISCO, the river which crosses central Brazil and the drought zone. Here Albuquerque Demosthenes Pessoà is leaving his fields of onions and peppers, arid desert three years ago, which a government irrigation scheme has enabled him to keep watered all day. This year, as last year, he hopes for two crops in 365 days.

TATA WORKS, 140 MILES FROM CALCUTTA · This enormous metallurgical plant smelts steel for the whole of India. At the mouth of the blast-furnaces, water is sprayed on the white-hot steel—4,000 gallons of water are needed to treat one single ton of steel.

DAKAR · It is ten o'clock. The public street fountains, which supply a population of 340,000, slowly peter out. They have been running for two hours and will be turned on for another two hours late in the evening. Each inhabitant, after a long wait in a queue, will have been supplied with 3 gallons for the day.

THE INDUS VALLEY, PAKISTAN · The Indus and its tributaries, the Jhelum, Chenab, Ravi, Beas and Sutlej, have deposited the rich soils of

the Punjab and Sindh. The rainfall is low but the rivers are large, and this has given such impetus to irrigation that the canal system extends for more than 40,000 miles and covers 25 million acres; irrigation everywhere, as far as the eye can see. Nothing comparable exists in the world and 30 million people are supported by it. But the canals have been cut in the bare soil, and 40 per cent of the water which circulates in them is absorbed while the fields are being irrigated. The level of the subterranean water-table has risen, and, in the absence of drainage, the evaporation of surface water has deposited a layer of mineral salts. Because of this, 100,000 acres a year are turned into swamp land or rendered sterile by the salts. According to experts from Harvard, twenty-five years and 2,000 million dollars will be needed to redress the situation.

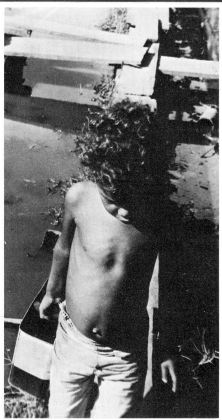

Bruges, where water seems abundant

Water seems plentiful in Rio de Janeiro, but it is polluted, and the clean fountain is often a long walk from home

Dakar—the daily search for water (opposite page)

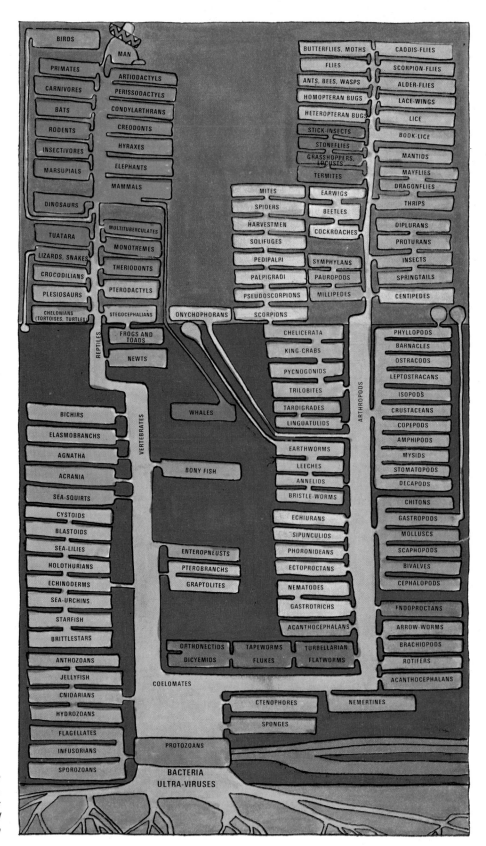

Family-tree of the animal kingdom, showing the links between water and man

CHAPTER 1

WATER IS THE ORIGIN OF LIFE

Water, which is so changeable and fluid, has nevertheless two characteristics to which we can cling today: its apparent permanence, and its quantity, which has remained the same for billions of years. Among all the questions raised, one thing is certain: that these same waters have for ever flowed, intermingled, swollen, merged with lakes and oceans, evaporated, fallen as rain, infiltrated and served as drink, as food for plants and as an aid to cooking, bakery and building. The water which cools the engine of a lorry running from Cologne to Hamburg could once have bathed Cleopatra.

Ocean formation

It has been postulated (H. Revelle) that the continuous exhalation of water-vapour from inside the earth gradually filled the ocean beds, said to have been formed some thousands of millions of years ago.

The origin of the ocean beds is also discussed by scientists a great deal. Some people say that the Pacific, which is as full of craggy heights and depths as the most uneven of mountain ranges, and the Atlantic, which is not so deep but is crossed by a sunken chain of mountains, were the result of the uneven way in which the earth solidified after it had been in a molten state. Large stretches of crust, already hardened on a still slimy planet, must have floated about, met, grouped together or broken up, and finally settled down after crashes, convulsions and shrinkage. One authority, Wegener, sees in this process a possible explanation for the way in which the earth settled, and which can be seen on planispheres—for instance, from the eastern shores of South America to the curve on the western side of Africa. Others, like Revelle and Von H. Petterson, think that the "sweating" of water in particular places during the last hundreds of millions of years, since the beginning of the Tertiary age, could, with volcanic eruptions, account for both the old upheavals in the beds of what today are the oceans, and their protuberances, such as the crags and folds in the earth's crust.

So, by means of these theories, we can explain the distribution of water on the earth—97 per cent of the total volume being taken up by the oceans.

It was in these oceanic depressions that life originated. Experiments in the laboratory have reconstituted this primitive environment and ultimately succeeded in synthesizing complex chemical sub-

East coast of
Greenland, showing
marks left on the
earth by ice

stances which were the forerunners of proteins. Thus life started in sea water.

The ultra-violet rays of the sun, rich in energy, then shone down continuously on the oceans. The water contained such large quantities of ammonia, methane and carbon dioxide—all the constituents necessary for the formation of those molecules found in living organisms —that these substances were able to combine and subdivide over hundreds of millions of years and finally to engender life. The long process of evolution began, from rudimentary organisms and plants down to man.

The aquatic origin of life is manifest in all the essential functions of vegetable matter, animals and human beings. Man himself is two-thirds water. Before birth he lies in a protective bag of water in his mother's womb, and water flows in his body until he dies; blood contains 79 per cent water. The whole animal kingdom is subject to this, and with a few exceptions the plants, themselves impregnated with water, take their nourishment from water and the atmosphere. Some of these phenomena have still not been satisfactorily explained. How, for example, does water rise to the top point of a pine tree 300 feet high? Whether we can see it or not, water, which initiated life, also perpetuates it.

Water sculpture

It was water, too, which shaped the earth. Glaciers have carved out the sharp mountain-faces and smoothed the peaks into the rounded shapes we see today. They have gouged out the valleys and the canyons, worn away basins for lakes, and broken off boulders to carry them down to the plains. Rocks and

pebbles from Scandinavia have been found in Britain as well as in Germany and the Soviet Union. The Finger Lakes of New York State are the work of glaciers, as are the sharp ridges of the Matterhorn in Switzerland.

For millions of years the earth was bitten, scratched and pummelled by the ice, then alternately rubbed, caressed and slapped by the roaring waters of springs, streams and rivers, which were less spectacular but marked it just as deeply, sculpting the landscapes of caves and valleys. Working hard, slowly and patiently, water cut deep valleys, broad or narrow, straight or winding, depositing silt as they spread out on to alluvial plains or formed a delta. In 4,500 years the delta of the Tigris and Euphrates has pushed forward the coast of the Persian Gulf 200 miles. Ephesus gave directly on to the sea when St Paul preached there; today the Meander has advanced the coast by about 12 miles, and winds through the valley in curves which it wears away on one side and builds up on the other. This process continues and will go on continuing; the ever-active water carves out its path before our very eyes and imperceptibly alters our landscapes.

Beneath the ground the ceaseless work of water is equally impressive. The grottoes and caves of Italy, France, Australia, Mexico and the eastern part of the United States bear witness that the Chinese torture of dripping water has an erosive effect.

On the ground the harmless-looking rain falls like miniature hammer-blows, stabbing and chopping; the soil is pierced full of holes, carved into channels and finally washed away. This is soil erosion, which impoverishes and destroys, demineralizes and leaves behind an

The fossil valleys of
the Sahara

The famous "wave"
of the cedar road,
in Lebanon

Cuenca: natural sculptures
made by water

inert soil on which nothing will grow.

The sea, which sculpted the cliffs of Etretat on the French coast and which eats away six feet a year from the shoreline of Nantucket Island in the United States, the sea, which erodes coasts and displaces sands, swallowing up one beach here to make another somewhere else, is, even so, less effective in its violence than the silky flow of rivers or the peaceful shower of rain. Lao-Tse remarked in the 10th century B.C.: "There is nothing in the world more inconsistent than water; it corrodes the hardest and strongest of substances; nothing can either resist or replace it."

The first ditch

Water mastered the earth, shaped it, gave rise to life ... and to man. Man then mastered, or tried to master, water. The first men set up their communities around water sources; it was over water supplies that they first came to blows, and it was in order to harness water that they first united and organized themselves. From the cave-dwelling to the lake-settlement, from rude dikes to rudimentary canals, the first ditch in the history of mankind was dictated by the demands for water. The siting of towns, the rhythm of work, the measurement of time, the gods, the types of dwelling, social organization and laws, public holidays and primitive technology, all were connected with water.

But it would be foolish and mistaken to think that early man grew and spread with the kindly help of water, for he was faced with constant changes and upheavals. The glaciers alternately grew larger or smaller, the oceans and seas subsided or increased and spread, lands appeared or were engulfed, and climates changed completely. Each time something like this happened, the part of the world involved would be transformed. While the glaciers encroached on the temperate regions, rain poured down on the subtropical regions and the tropical zones became smaller; but when the ice withdrew, the temperate regions reappeared and the rains spread there, while deserts were found in places that had once been well-watered. Flora and fauna altered to suit these changed conditions, forests vanished from one place and appeared elsewhere, and so did plant-eating animals, while rivers, streams and lakes grew smaller or larger as the springs dried up or flourished.

Later, when the violent changes ceased and milder conditions prevailed, men were constantly on the move, settling temporarily according to the rhythm of the water and its seasons. In one place they would wait for the salmon to come tumultuously upriver in the cold weather; in another, they managed to cross a water-way; in another, they used stone *bolas* (stones tied to the end of a thong, still used in Latin America) to catch animals swimming in the water and drown them; farther away, beside sea or ocean, they collected molluscs: mussels and oysters. Shell-fish, collected not only for their food value but for their beauty or bright colour, were probably the earliest form of money.

Civilization was born in four great aquatic basins—the warm valleys of the Yellow River, the Tigris and Euphrates, the Nile and the Indus. We are reminded daily of this origin; it was upon the annual flooding of the Nile that the Egyptians calculated the calendar of 365 days.

Historians have established 5000 B.C. as the date of the development of the lower Yellow River valley, when it was drained to dry up the swamps and the forests were cleared. A stream of capricious moods, now sluggish, now turbulent, frozen over for several months, the Yellow River nevertheless submitted to the pattern of irrigation and navigation canals which the Chinese imposed on it.

The Mesopotamian civilization emerged from the swamps of the

Archimedes, who was interested in all forms of movement, and therefore in water. Engraving in Thevet's Hommes illustres

The Nile temple of Abu Simbel—recently moved because of water engineering

More watermarks on the landscape: signs of glaciers and of gradual erosion through water. This is the river Jucar y Cuenca, in New Castille

The circus of Navacelles in the Herault

Tigris-Euphrates delta. Despite unstable and treacherous rivers, rebellious by nature, several large Mesopotamian towns had established networks of canals by 3000 B.C.

A little later the Nile delta was supporting the third of these great civilizations. Towards the end of the 4th millennium B.C. the Egyptians had controlled part of the river and its inundations, by containing it, running off its waters, diverting it,

and by making ditches, reservoirs and rudimentary canals. The Nile, friendly and generous, timing its rise regularly each year at the end of June and subsiding at the end of October, deposited a layer of rich, fertile ooze, and thus favoured this development.

The Indus showed no sign of community development until about 2500 B.C., but when this happened it was on a larger scale

Snow bridge under the waterfall in the Vanoise massif, Isère

The effects of water, seen between Teruel and Ademuz in Spain

A relic of early civilization: the colossus of Memnon, Egypt . . .

. . . and the temple of Karnak, at Luxor

and in many ways more technically advanced. Mohenjo-Daro boasted a number of two-storey private houses provided with a bathroom and main drainage. Waste water from each house was led to a covered central sewer which carried it to sumps or pits.

For the people who had learned to sow and plant, water provided the living force which multiplied the crops. Nobody could yet understand how or why; therefore water assumed the nature of a god. How these beliefs arose many centuries before Christ is depicted in the following quotations: "Over all the Gods reigns Enki, the Absolute, the Unfathomable, from whom everything emanates. From 'Enki' (primordial water) two secondary gods derive, 'Apsou' (fresh water) and 'Tiamat' (salt water). These three gods united form the Trinity (one God in three persons) from which all living beings, including man and the other gods,[1] have emanated." And again—"WATER is the primordial force of LIFE. Combined with Osiris (the sun), the force which releases LIFE, it gives rise to Kâ (the spirit)."[2]

Early irrigation

Of necessity, it was water for farming that first took up people's energy. As the Nile overflowed in Egypt there was no problem, but in its lower reaches it required hard, slow, exhausting work to irrigate the fields. It was probably in Mesopotamia, in the 1st millennium B.C., that a solution was found in the form of the *shadouf*, which very soon passed into Egypt as well. At Luxor, on the steep river-bank opposite the temple of Karnak and up against the Valley of the Kings, I saw men working a *shadouf* a couple of years ago. A forked stick, stuck into the rich river-bank, held a long, thin wooden rod balanced on it; at one end of the rod—the shorter piece—was a weight made of dried earth, and at the other end was a leather container. One of the men raised the counter-weight until the container was in the water. When he dropped it, the filled container rose slowly. The second man, standing on the bank, then poured the water into a canal that took it, through a number of channels, to the fields. Two men working like this could, I was told, raise over 650 gallons of water a day from river or canal and pour it over the fields, just as they did three thousand years ago.

We have to wait several centuries for the next step. The inventor, who remains as anonymous as the inventor of the *shadouf*, conceived the idea of fixing around the circumference of a wheel a series of vessels which filled with water as they passed beneath the surface of the river and then emptied themselves into an irrigation channel. The process was repeated in continuous motion and was worked by men treading the bars of a kind of squirrel's cage. A variation of this system, using an ox or an ass instead of slaves to turn the wheel endlessly round in the water and bring the water up several feet, spread all over the Mediterranean, and today is still used in Egypt and in Spain, where it is known as the *noria*.

Archimedes of Syracuse deserves the fame which has followed him down to the present day for inventing the endless screw which bears his name. A heavy, hollow cylinder made of wood is plunged into the water; inside it is another cylinder, with a thin spiral band from top to

[1] The Gods of Sumer (5th and 4th millennium B.C.).

[2] Egyptian hieroglyphs (3rd millennium B.C.).

bottom, and this is turned on its axis by a winch. The water is brought up by each rising turn of the spiral. Often in the morning Egyptian children set off on their small donkeys with the cylinder lying on their knees, and make for some small or far-away field where a *shadouf* or a *noria* is of little value.

Moving water from its regular channels, therefore, was the first object, and these were the earliest techniques.

The original canals

A text inscribed on the pyramids of the VI dynasty says: "They trembled when they saw the waves of Hapi (the Nile) coming, but soon they were laughing, for the riverbanks bloomed, the gifts of the gods came down from heaven, men offered homage and the heart of the gods was gladdened." Too much or too little water for farming brought famine and suffering, however: dikes and canals quickly became a dominant preoccupation. Stabilization of water supply in order to ensure that this transient nourishment was always at hand, and its transfer to localities where it could

be used to increase the area of fertile land—these were urgent necessities. Life depended on it.

Long before the time of Menès, founder of the first dynasty of the kings of Egypt in 3100 B.C., upper and lower Egypt were criss-crossed by a network of dikes and canals. The whole social organization of the country was centred on these frail lifelines of the soil.

Water can be a nuisance, and even dangerous, as well as beneficial

The reappearance of the Loue river, in the Jura Mountains

Water-worship: bathing in the holy
Ganges at Benares

Zagorsk, a religious centre in the
U.S.S.R. where there is a miraculous
spring

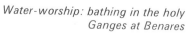

The temple of Tirta Empul, in Bali
(right, above)

Bali: annual purification ceremony
(right, below)

The tenuous canals of the early days were transformed into complex systems and later into navigation routes, a new development for water. Without it the pyramids could never have been built. The Chinese connected practically all their rivers by means of canals, and the whole system culminated in the monumental Grand Canal, which runs down from Peking to Hangchow, a length of 1,000 miles, part of which is still in service. The Egyptians, who had doubled and then tripled the Nile by means of a network of canals, had the further audacity to join the river to the Red Sea with a canal as early as 600 B.C. Europe and then the United States rediscovered this method of utilizing water as a practical means of communication when the fever of the Industrial Revolution seized England in the 18th century.

The water-clock

From Greece to Rome the same things were happening; water, which had given life to civilization, was extending its bounds and providing a unifying influence.

Water fascinated people; then it puzzled them. Could it serve no other purpose than that of quenching the thirst of men, beasts and fields? Already its nature and its possibilities teemed with questions. Thus, in Egypt, was born the waterclock—the clepsydra. A jar perforated with one or more holes was filled with a measured quantity of water (the earliest forms of measure were measures of water), and the time it took to run out served as a unit of time. The same system regulated the length of pleas before the Greek tribunals. But a great step forward in the use of water was the discovery of its energy.

The epigram of Antipates of Thessalonika re-creates for us the wonder of the ancients, which resembled that of the modern world when confronted with the phenomenon of atomic energy. "Women, up till now busy at grinding your corn, tire your arms no longer, sleep on in the morning and let the cock crow in vain to announce the dawn. Ceres has ordered her nymphs to take over the work of your hands; they have rushed to the wheels to turn the axle and this, helped by the spokes which surround it, drives four heavy millstones. *The Golden Age is born again for us*, for without labour or exertion we can enjoy the gifts of Ceres."

The use of water for industrial purposes probably goes back to the 2nd millennium B.C., when the first wheel was put into the water in Illyria and its blades were set in motion by the current. As they turned they moved the hollow grindstones, thus releasing women from the necessity of getting up at cockcrow.

The next step was to stand the wheel up instead of letting it lie flat, and to make it run vertically. Several turns of the millstones now corresponded with one turn of the

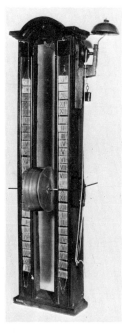

wheel—more corn ground in less time.

It is said to have been Ctesibius who, in 135 B.C., had the idea of improving the water-wheel by replacing blades with buckets.

The Industrial Revolution

Once the movement to use water for industrial purposes was launched, it became progressively more important. Paddles replaced buckets, and, in the 14th century, Candidus Benignus built a mill near Arles powered by sixteen paddle-wheels—a remarkable achievement for its time. In Europe, from the 18th century onwards, water-power was used to work blacksmiths' hammers, flour-mills, and all kinds of cutting tools; later it was used in the cloth and paper industries and in sawmills.

A major change in man's attitude to water came when he stopped concentrating on water for agriculture and switched to harnessing it for industry.

The Industrial Revolution in the 18th century sealed the fate of the water-wheel. The invention by Watt of his steam-engine in 1763, following on the discoveries of Denis Papin and Thomas Newcomen, pro-

Water-wheel still in use in Majorca

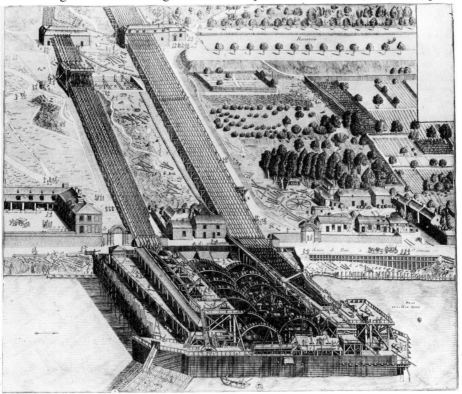

Water-powered machine at Marly (engraving —Paris, Bibliothèque Nationale)

Recife: the lake-town next to the factory

vided the human race with the means for rapid development. But it was still water, this time in the form of vapour, which enabled him to do so through its exceptional properties. Water becomes steam at only a moderate temperature, but it absorbs a great deal of heat, a lot of energy, in changing itself into vapour. Conversely, in changing from steam to the liquid state, it releases a large quantity of thermal energy. This energy is the source of power in a steam-engine; transformed into mechanical energy, it can equally well be used to drive a pump or a ship.

This, then, was the Steam Revolution, brought about thanks to water, which expands to about 1,600 times its original volume when it vaporizes. We only need to take Britain as an example. In 1870 the capacity of steam-engines in use in the United Kingdom was equal to the work performed by 40 million men. The country could only have provided enough bread to feed a third of these fictitious workers.

Water has never lost the promise which it held in those early days.

Its great complexity always provides scope for the discovery of new possibilities and for more economic use of its well-established characteristics. The great dams with their hydro-electric installations derive the power for their generators from water; so water faces successfully the challenges offered by new discoveries, and electricity has only enhanced its importance. The Hoover Dam in the United States, that at Bratsk in Siberia, at Aswan in Egypt, all bear witness, indisputable but often forgotten, to the power and importance of water.

Water, which yesterday nurtured the birth of civilization, is today closely involved with the problems of the modern world.

First man struggled against water; then he harnessed it, and struggled with it; finally he had to struggle to find it.

Water was a cause of fighting: men have died for the bank of a river or the source of a stream. The many boundaries which pass along the courses of rivers bear witness to this. The richest part of the

vocabulary of any language deals with water in all its forms: lagoon, lake, steam, spring, leat, ice, fluid, jet, wave . . . how many words does a "dictionary of water" contain?

Water has left its mark on the earliest civilizations, formed the basis of our calendar, instituted gods and laws, and set up for its utilization the earliest form of public administration and the first officials who supervised the Nile inundations and collected the dues from each user. It has shaped our landscapes and our climate, it provides us with electricity, and it is simultaneously in our blood and in the clouds. . . .

*House on the water
in South-East Asia*

*The aqueduct at
Tarragona, Spain*

CHAPTER 2

THE SECRETS
OF WATER

The formula for water given in books of elementary chemistry, H_2O, embodies one of the most complex chemical substances and one of the most difficult to obtain in the pure state. It is full of anomalies in its physical properties, exceptional in its formation, and inconsistent to the point that many of its effects on other substances are still unexplained, as for example dissolution, ionization, hydrolysis and hydration. Whenever its structure is investigated a new discovery seems to come to light. Water occurs in solid, liquid and gaseous form of which only one, solid ice, is less dense than liquid water.

Water is commonplace, odourless, colourless and tasteless, yet at the same time unique, fantastic and exceptional. Although its nutritive value is practically nil, it is the principal constituent of all living creatures. It is a poor electrolyte, yet paradoxically it can ionize and dissolve a host of substances. Certain types of matter contain no water, yet can give it off when heated; others which contain plenty will only release it at 1200°C. The blue component of "sympathetic ink" contains only three molecules of water, but the slightest excess of moisture decomposes it and makes it turn rose-coloured. Water rusts iron, but by contrast iron will decompose water if it is sufficiently hot. It is repelled by almost all organic substances, but is strongly attracted by the majority of mineral compounds, also by itself. When it freezes, water increases in volume; it swells instead of contracting like most other substances. Solid, it floats upon its liquid self. It can absorb or liberate more heat than the majority of known substances, but its boiling point as well as its freezing point are exceptions to the general rule. A remarkably stable chemical, a powerful solvent and an important source of energy, water is unique.

What fascinated the ancients was not the mere substance of water. Each of its often unique characteristics forms one of the components which weave the fabric of our existence, from the process of digestion to the control of climate or the extraction of sulphur. To investigate the intimate aspects of its structure we must approach it as a miscellany known as water.

Composition of water

It would appear that the molecular structure of water, two atoms of hydrogen to one of oxygen (H_2O), can explain a number of its special properties, although the formula, H_2O, is far from perfect. The water we call natural (i.e., untouched by

The force and violence of water in the Oisans mountain region

A molecule of water

Chemical analysis of water in a laboratory at the water-purification plant at Corbeil-Essones

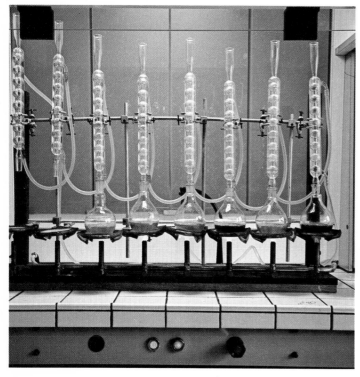

man) always carries solids and gases dissolved in it, so the formula does not fully describe the contents. This same water purified—emptied and clear of other things—becomes even more complex. It is a mixture, as far as we know today, of 18 bodies, among them 3 of hydrogen (protium, deuterium and tritium) and 3 of oxygen; so now the formula does no more than describe water's basic make-up.

Even today water remains a mysterious compound, and two centuries ago it was considered incapable of being broken up into its constituent parts.

It was the English physicist Cavendish who, in 1783, demolished this belief by proving experimentally that hydrogen and oxygen unite to form water when exposed to an electric spark. In 1785, Laplace and Meunier supported this evidence by proceeding the other way round and decomposing water on a red-hot iron, thus crudely establishing what everyone knows today, that 18 parts of water decompose into 16 parts of oxygen and 2 parts of hydrogen. Humboldt, Gay-Lussac and Avogadro all continued to make discoveries about water and its structure, and with each fresh discovery new problems arose. This is still true today.

The analysis of water—this omnipresent, multiform water that has marked the face of the earth and the development of man—is, it has been found, at the basis of the essential laws of our modern-day chemistry.

Varieties of water

What kind of water are we talking about? Today we distinguish between water of constitution, water of crystallization, water of insertion, water moisture, and water that is physiologically linked with organs and tissues.

C. Duval expresses this unequivocally, using seeds as an example, when he says (note our emphasis): "When dehydration is carried out without weighing the water, the weight of the substance must be determined before and after the operation. Although *conventionally* water possesses a tension of one atmosphere at 100°, there is no general rule that fixes the temperature of dehydration of a substance for certain, *because there are various kinds of water*. The time needed to eject it depends not only on the temperature, but even more on the size of the seeds, their weight, the thickness of the layer, the shape of the jar in which they are exposed, the speed with which they are heated up, and the speed of the current of air in the apparatus."

Today we are a long way from the fine, reassuring simplicity of the old beliefs about water.

We have to go back to first principles, then, in order to try to explain water and its often curious behaviour, and then to give concrete examples which will illustrate them, up to a point, each exception to the general rule involving a complementary rule or showing us that there is an unknown one.

Water is a particularly stable body, which frees a large amount of heat when it is formed and decomposes at a very high temperature: the atoms of hydrogen and oxygen strongly oppose being separated and quickly come together again, in both cases freeing a great deal of energy. A large amount of energy is needed to divide them, and an equally large amount to bring them together again. Sokoloff, for instance, using a current of 5 milliampères, had to wait several months to decompose water in this way. In order to hasten the separation in industry, a solution of soda is added to the water; but, even then, it takes from 12 to 14 kilowatt-hours to obtain 35 cubic feet of oxygen and 70 cubic feet of hydrogen.

As they combine so readily, however, atoms of oxygen and hydrogen nevertheless free a considerable amount of energy; this is already used in space-satellites, and perhaps

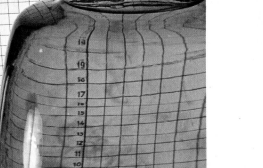

Water clings to itself and around itself

Solution of permanganate

31

may soon power electric cars that will not pollute the air.

"Cat's head"

In shape and appearance, a molecule of water is asymmetrical—lop-sided, and with gaps in it. The two atoms of hydrogen are on the same side, at an angle of about 105°—rather like ears on the round head of a cat whose mouth is the atom of oxygen! But the electrons that link them are nearer to the "mouth" than the ears, so that the proton of hydrogen, exposed and with a small electrostatic attraction, allows the whole to be linked with a long series of compounds. That is what is called the "hydrogen bond".

The molecule of water, which is strongly linked to other water molecules, is at the same time open, with the ability both to penetrate and carry.

This means that water is the universal solvent for solids, even of salts of silver. It dissolves them with variations and changes, as always happens wherever there is water. Some are dissolved weight for weight, which seems strange at first sight, but can be checked in the laboratory. The temperature, too, plays a part in what happens, which may seem puzzling, but is a fact. Much odder still is the fact that some salts, like sodium sulphate, are much more soluble cold than hot. Pressure also has an influence: 68·1 per cent potassium nitrate, for instance, dissolves under a pressure of one atmosphere whereas no more than 25·3 per cent dissolves under a hundred atmospheres.

Among all these confusing special examples, there is one series of absolute rules: the dissolving of a substance in water lowers the point of freezing or compressibility, and increases the viscosity, or stickiness, and artificial tension. If two substances are dissolved, this is no longer true: the more the solubility of the two is lowered, the more it is improved. Water is full of surprises. The most amazing thing about it is this: although water is the universal solvent for solids, it will dissolve only certain liquids—alcohols, for instance, and never oils—and certain gases, such as air, nitrogen and carbonic gas. Water also plays two of these rôles at once, or else one after the other: for instance, there is its distillation at less than 100 per cent, which holds and restores the scent of jasmine or violet without altering it.

Life on earth would be impossible if water were not a powerful solvent, stronger as far as solids are concerned than it is for liquids or gases, and able to carry in it almost half the chemical elements known at the present time.

It is this property that allows the chemist to prepare a remarkable range of products by combining reactions and deriving hydrogen and ammonia, as in the production of fertilizers or household gas. Without water, how would we wash the earth off our vegetables, and how, in its turn, would we wash the pesticides out of the soil? How could we build without cement, mortar or plaster, or without bricks, tiles and modern mixed materials—without, in fact, the water that dissolves and binds and carries? And above all, how could we provide ourselves with food without water? All living organisms, plant and animal, need water to dissolve and bring them the substances they need. It is water that, through their roots, brings nourishment from the soil, once it has been dissolved, to the grain of wheat or the flower.

It is water, once again, that dissolves and dilutes the flour in baking,

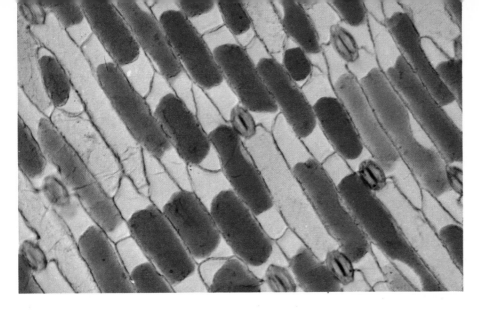

Plasmolization of a tulip cell

and thus makes it possible for us to enjoy our daily bread.

Water also carries gases, carbon dioxide, mineral salts and organic matter. R. Furon and I. Cheret both emphasize this fact—something so ordinary and long-accepted that we rarely give it a thought, although it permits animal and plant life to exist together in the watery realm. Billions of microscopic beings swarm over the beds of rivers and lakes, living in the water and through the water. In turn they influence the chemical composition of the water, particularly the amount of oxygen, carbon dioxide, sulphur, phosphorus and nitrogen which it con-

tains; and when they die, these microscopic creatures form deposits at the bottom of the river or lake upon which the fishes feed.

Because water is a solvent, and can carry so much within itself too, life in the watery realm is intensely active; its balance is always changing, the death of one kind of life meaning life for another kind, the waste from one sort being food for another variety. Rivers and seas are thus endlessly cleaning components dissolved by water—so long as the natural processes and balance are not disturbed by human pollution.

The physical properties of water, which we exploit every day in our

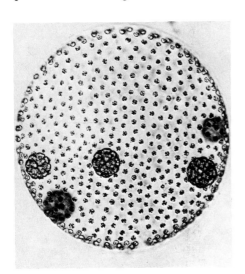

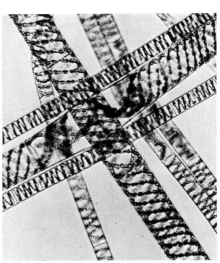

The fresh-water alga coenobe (Volvox aureus) with plant multiplication, enlarged 350 times

Fresh-water alga spirogyrus, enlarged 250 times

An industrial cooler

under pressure it becomes less—which is the opposite of what happens with other liquids; its surface tension and its surface energy do not behave like those of normal liquids, either. In other words, water is a relative thing, with nothing certain, firm and constant about it.

It is the specific heat of water that defines the calorie (a calorie is the amount needed to heat a kilogramme of water from freezing point to 1°C), but this varies like everything else involved. It is only convention that allows us to set down any exact figures, such as the degree, which is defined as a hundredth of the difference between the moment when water solidifies and becomes ice at 0°C, and the moment when it boils and becomes vapour at 100°C. It must be made clear that the ice obtained at 0°C is the only ordinary ice—the only kind that is lighter than liquid water and less dense.

Without a doubt water, which was used to measure time in Ancient Egypt and through which we now measure weight and degrees, has curious relationships with heat and cold.

When the temperature goes down, nearly all bodies, whether solid, liquid or gaseous, contract and become denser. As far as 4°C, and only that far, water follows this rule. Below 4°C it does not; it starts to swell and become less dense; and when water solidifies at 0°C, to become ice, snow or frost, depending on the situation, it becomes even less dense and, even more extraordinary, increases its volume by about one-eleventh.

This anomaly is both beneficent and disastrous. It is beneficent because if solidified water did not float —if ice, in fact, did not float on top of the water which formed it and carries it, but flowed—our world

domestic or industrial life, also seem odd in a number of ways. Water is colourless and tasteless—it seems self-effacing enough to vanish before our very eyes; yet it is so independent and has such special qualities that it cannot be compared with anything else or even be exactly described.

The density of water (maximum at 4°C under normal pressure) is one of the lowest in the metric system. Indeed, more and more delicate and exact measurements set its maximum density at 3·982°C, and its density at 0·99997 grammes per cubic centimetre. It is rather ironical to find so changeable a thing as water measured so precisely.

The more we examine water's characteristics, the more anomalies appear: its viscosity changes, and

The violence of a storm — Valenciennes (1750–1819)

would have become a white, congealed desert. Lakes, streams and rivers would have been silted up, with the ice at the bottom of them, and this ice-silting would have become progressively thicker; and the ice-caps, instead of breaking up into icebergs that float across the oceans and finally melt in milder climates, would have taken over the depths, gradually solidifying the Arctic and Antarctic regions, and extending their grip relentlessly outwards. Although this may seem a far-fetched idea, it does serve to illustrate the importance of every one of the ambiguous qualities found in water. The same quality may, of course, spell disaster for water-pipes, car radiators, central-heating installations, or boats which become trapped in lakes or rivers. With water, you can expect advantages and disadvantages, good luck and bad!

This volatile quality is explained by the "dancing" way in which the molecules of water are linked, each atom of oxygen being co-ordinated four times to four other atoms, with an atom of hydrogen inserted. This series of four-pointed stars that spreads a close-knit, moving pattern in liquid water stops only at the edges, the surface and the bottom of the water. When water becomes solid, the "dance" of the atoms congeals, the flexible, moving patterns become fixed, and the molecules which were twisting and interchanging are kept still, at a distance from one another. As the whole thing

A dried-up river-bed, Haiti

increases in size, it becomes aerated, turning into a hollow, porous thing with a hexagonal pattern; the molecules, which had been twirling in fours, whipping at one another with their flexible antennae, are now held where they are by stiffened antennae, and the same number of molecules takes up more room.

This all happens in principle at 0°C, because if liquid water is subjected to ultra-sonic radiation, it will not congeal before it has reached −30°C.

Water boils at 100°C; this also seems abnormal. The boiling point of water should be under 63·5°C, if it followed other examples—in other words, if the molecule of water was a single one and water was a simple body.

However, it is lucky for us that water does boil at 100°C (and at 84°C on the top of Mont Blanc) for otherwise we should have only light vapour on the earth. Better still, water is a poor and irregular conductor of heat, and it is only after it has received a good deal of energy that we get water-vapour. Anyone who has burnt himself with a kettle or a saucepan knows that you can get blisters long before the water starts simmering. This is because water is extremely slow to heat up. Essentially this is because taking a liquid to boiling point means incorporating in it the energy that sets its molecules in motion, and because the molecules of water, being strongly formed and strongly moved, need a great deal of energy to be divided. This is why water is used in radiators and in order to cool industrial

plants: it absorbs a great deal of heat before it becomes heated even a little.

On the other hand, water is also slow to cool. The metal of the saucepan or the radiator heats much faster than the water, but the metal will have cooled when the water is still warm. This capacity to absorb heat, or heat capacity, used in industry and in everyday life, is completed by the latent heat of water, which is also abnormally high.

Latent heat, which is considerable, varies, it is said, between 539 and 540 calories at 100°C, and at 0°C it is about 595 calories. If it is borne in mind that latent heat has been given its name because it brings about no change of temperature, but merely alters the form of the substance, then it will be clear how important this high latency is in the changeable behaviour of water. Every liquid, when it is heated, stops for a while at boiling point to absorb the heat, without changing its temperature, exclusively in order to turn into gas. Water is particularly greedy at such a moment, and this explains why a veranda or a balcony which has become overheated is sprinkled with water: as evaporation takes place, it takes the calories from the surrounding air and cools it.

This high latent heat, which uses calories to give us a cup of coffee, is also the great regulator of our climate: oceans, seas, lakes, rivers and streams all absorb and free heat, lessening the differences in temperature between day and night, and between times of great heat and bitter cold.

Luxuriant growth in Thailand

CHAPTER 3

WATER OPERATES EVERYWHERE

An adult man in good health contains from 58 to 66 per cent of water, about two-thirds of his weight. If he is thin, his percentage of water can reach 70 per cent, but if he tends to be on the well-fed side it drops to 55 per cent. Fat people have a lower water content.

But, plump or thin, water remains his principal constituent, a fact which is even more apparent during gestation; 97 per cent of water in a three-day-old human embryo, 94 per cent in a foetus of three months.

Water invades all human tissues; it flows along our 60 miles of veins and arteries, floats between the interstices of living cells, occupies our intestinal and ocular cavities, the hollow part of bones and tendons; it circulates in the anatomy and beats with the heart.

In the brain, the centre of all human consciousness, there is 74·5 per cent of water.

Man is saturated with water from head to foot; 98 per cent of water in tears, 79 per cent in blood, 10 per cent in the teeth, 79·3 per cent in the heart, 79·1 per cent in the lungs, 70 per cent in the liver, 77 per cent in the intestines, 76 per cent in the muscles, and 22 per cent in the skeletal structure. And his outer covering of skin itself is constituted of 72 per cent water.

Animals, too, are saturated with water. The jellyfish holds the record with 95·41 per cent, almost the same as sea water, while the chicken, dog, rabbit and the cat, like the mouse which it chases, average around 67 per cent, a little more than the water content of an adult man.

When it becomes a slice of ham, the pig contains 72·5 per cent of water, and a bullock in the form of steak 76·4 per cent. A roast of veal has 78·4 per cent and a pullet 74·2 per cent. The fishmonger's mackerel carries 71·2 per cent, a fresh herring 74·6 per cent, a sole 79·2 per cent and an eel 57·4 per cent.

Man's intake of nourishment is composed essentially of water, even though he may not know it. Vegetables are full of it, and those we eat daily are oozing with it; 93 per cent in the heart of an artichoke, 89·6 per cent in a carrot, 90 per cent in a cauliflower, 75·8 per cent in a Spanish onion, 78 per cent in potatoes, 95·6 per cent in lettuce and 91·01 per cent in tomatoes. And ordinary wheat bread, though baked at a temperature of 100°C., contains even then 33·7 per cent of water.

Fruit, too, soaks in the same bath —87 per cent of water in the pineapple, between 75 and 80 per cent

A rainbow

Location	Volume of water (Cubic miles)	Percentage of Total
WATER RESERVES OF THE WORLD		
SURFACE		
Fresh water lakes	30.000	0·009
Salt lakes and inland seas	25,000	0·008
Rivers and water-courses	300	0·0001
UNDERGROUND		
Humidity in the soil	16,000	0·005
Subterranean water at a depth of less than 2,600 feet	1,000,000	0·31
Deep subterranean water	1,000,000	0·31
Ice-caps and glaciers	7,000,000	2·15
Atmosphere	3,100	0·001
Oceans	317,000,000	97·2

in the lemon, orange, grapefruit, apple, strawberry and raspberry. The water which the human organism needs is given it not only by drinks, but by the thirsty animal and vegetable life man consumes.

Ubiquitous water

So, water is everywhere, even in certain rocks like opal, asbestos and gypsum, and in freestone and slate, which lose it after being quarried and become difficult to work.

It covers almost 75 per cent of the earth's surface, taking the form of oceans, glaciers, lakes, streams and rivers, which add up to a total volume of 324 million cubic miles of water. Furthermore, there are 2 million cubic miles circulating or lying dormant underground, and finally more than 3,000 cubic miles are suspended in the atmosphere, chiefly in the form of vapour.

Everywhere water is on the move —from soil to plant, from plant to the atmosphere or to the animal

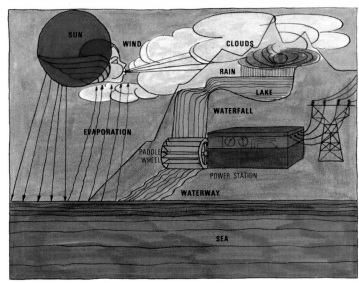

which feeds on it, from the animal to man for his nourishment, from the mountain to the sea via rivers and streams, from the cloud over the sea to the spring breaking through the ground, in the storm and in the blinking of an eye. Raymond Nace, hydrologist to the U.S. Geological Survey, has made a study of the various stages of this movement (see page 40).

(see page 40)

The Roman Vitruvius, around the year A.D. 90, was the first to suggest that evaporation, clouds and rain were all linked together in a continuous chain. But there were no concrete proofs, and it was not until the middle of the 17th century that two Frenchmen, Perrault and Mariotte, found some. Each separately measured the rainfall in the Seine basin, and then the amount of water that came out at the river's mouth. The figures balanced, when a margin was included to take in springs and wells. For the first time it had been proved that rainfall in a river basin was enough to feed the river.

Mariotte's further researches then showed that rain water seeped into the soil, passed through the porous levels of it, and finally collected on the impermeable layers. The endless chain was nearly established, and it was Edmund Halley who supplied the final link. He proved, with figures, that the amount of water evaporated by the Mediterranean was equivalent to the precipitation that fell on the shores around it. So, Perrault and Mariotte having proved that rain reappears as rivers and streams, and Halley's own experiments having established that evaporation from a sea balances the flow of rivers into it, he came to the conclusion that the same amount of water is in constant circulation.

The endless cycle of the drop of water which only leaves the earth in order to come back again and travels

The transformation cycle of a drop of water

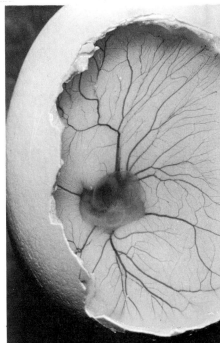

Development of a chick in the egg, in a watery solution, on the fifth day

Man's position in the centre of water-supplied energy

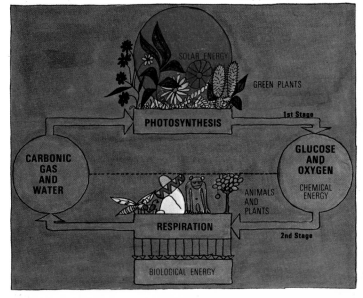

via plants, animals, men, rivers, streams, the sea, clouds, snow or rain, has since been more accurately measured. This perpetual circulation without beginning or end has been weighed, calculated, dissected and totalled. According to M. Mary and A. Janod, for a pump powered by the sun to work at any time, an average of 12 cubic miles of water an hour is evaporated, 10 of which rise from the oceans and 2 from the continents. And, according to the same calculation, all the water contained in the atmosphere is renewed, on average, 30 times a year—about every twelve days.

For the amount of water that falls is equivalent to the amount evaporated, giving the same figure of 12 cubic miles an hour, of which 9 come down on the oceans and 3 on the continents; but at this point the cycle ceases to be like a mechanical toy, carrying out precisely the same routine, time after time.

Twelve cubic miles are evaporated every hour, 10 from the oceans and 2 from the continents, and 12 fall every hour, but 9 on the oceans and 3 on the continents. The whole amount balances up, but the balance is upset if you look at it in more detail: the oceans lose 10 cubic miles per hour and get only 9 back, whereas the continents evaporate 2 cubic miles per hour and get back 3 in the same time. The conclusion is perfectly clear, however: 1 cubic mile reaches the oceans, either by flowing on the surface through streams and rivers, or else by seeping underground to feed the springs—the large hidden reservoirs and underground sheets of water.

The same water travels everywhere —a dozen days in the atmosphere, two or three weeks in a river, a century in a glacier, 100 to 30,000 years underground . . . and about twenty days in a man.

But the balance is purely global. New York and Paris neither receive nor evaporate the same amount of water, England has fogs which are unknown in Italy, and the hurricanes of Florida do not beset Germany. Evaporation and precipitation vary from one continent to another, between one nation and its neighbour and between regions, and the brightness of the sun, the force of winds, the structure of the soil exhibit differences which combine to ensure general equilibrium.

The general cycle of water is modified by special conditions and local variations, but achieves an overall balance in the end.

Rain and snow

Precipitated water is much more inconsistent than absorbed water. On land, at places a few miles apart, the quantities of rain or snow can easily vary by multiples of two or even four and six. Raindrops which sometimes swell to as much as 0·25 inch in diameter and weigh up to 0·75 ounce only produce one inch of annual rainfall at Suez, while in Cherrapunji, at the foot of the Himalayas, the annual measurement exceeds 470 inches. Irregularities of terrain prevent uniform distribution. A wind takes up humidity from the sea, cools as it rises up a mountain-side and discharges its condensation in the form of rain or snow. Descending the other slope, it dries the ground as it replenishes itself with more humidity. On the seas, where these irregularities of terrain do not exist, precipitation is much more uniform.

This cycle presupposes continual exchanges of heat during the whole of the journey of the drop of water which is evaporated from the ocean, subsequently travels thousands of miles in the form of vapour or droplets before returning to its original state and falling back to earth, there to run on the surface or sink into it before returning to the ocean. While circulating and changing its state it carries, absorbs or emits heat, thus stabilizing temperatures, reducing their variation and

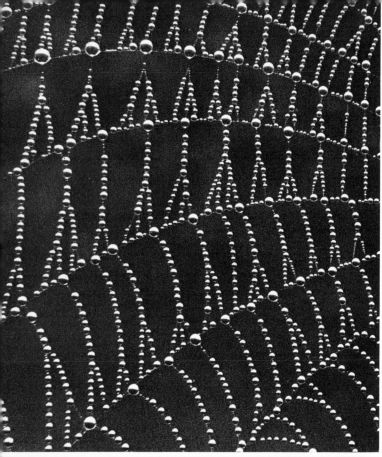

moderating them at points where the degree of heat or cold would become acute without its multiform and constant covering. As they travel the drops of water bring the warmth of the tropics to northern climes and the coolness of the Arctic to the equatorial zone.

It also regularizes temperatures by joining ocean currents or rivers, warm or cold, tropical or polar, which move about between continents and whose powerful waters help or harm the countries along their shores. The people of Siberia blame the cold current of the Bering Straits for the ice that blocks the sea routes and the ports, and makes the territory of Kamchatka uninhabitable. The people of Brittany are glad that the Gulf Stream warms their climate and allows them to gather early crops in the Morbihan area, whereas Labrador, which is on the same latitude but on the opposite side of the Atlantic, and which does not benefit from the Gulf Stream, has no vegetation.

Under the impetus of the sun, the wandering drop of water produces rain and shine, climates and marine currents, carves out valleys and constructs deltas, refreshes us in summer and warms us in cold weather. And every day it expends energy greater than any produced by man in the whole of his history.

"World Weather Watch"

The catalogue of our knowledge is extensive but it remains incomplete, and study of the movement of water, its temperature, rainfall and its behaviour has been taken up by scholars, research workers and technicians all over the world. Its temperature is taken on the surface of the ocean or in its depths three times a day for months on end; daily

measurements are taken of rainfall, degree of solar radiation and evapo-transpiration. I have already told this story of international co-operation, but it is not well known enough and, as an excellent example of its kind, it deserves to be remembered, commented upon and praised. In Paris, New York, London, Rome and Moscow the daily figures are collated for drawing up maps of rain or snow, or of temperature and humidity of soil and atmosphere. All these observations are finally assembled at the World Meteorological Organization (WMO), a department of UNO having its headquarters at Geneva, and the chief centre of the "World Weather Watch". Already Paris, London, Moscow, New York, New Delhi and Melbourne exchange their national data every morning, and draughtsmen trace planispheres on which the water-content of clouds, the density of rain and the rate of evaporation over land areas allow future weather to be forecast. Typhoons and tornadoes are foreseen and announced, and populations under threat are given immediate warning so that they can take shelter.

Space satellites have revolutionized and improved analytical observation of this part of the circulation of water. When Tiros I, launched in the United States on 1st April 1960, began to give information on the movement of water in the atmosphere over half a continent, earthbound observers, bent upon noting the day-to-day fluctuations of a cycle which was often subject to unexplained local disturbances, felt that a veil had been lifted and that a great step forward had been taken. In 1964 Moscow and Washington inaugurated a special line for the transmission of cloud diagrams provided by the

Scarcity of water kills, and the parched earth shrinks in a drought

The beauty of water: on a spider's web . . .

. . . or on the bonnet of a car

When there is water the earth blooms — a Brazilian forest near the waterfalls of Iguazù

satellites. Since then, the WMO has co-ordinated a programme which takes 100,000 observations per day from the earth and 11,000 from the atmosphere, with the help of 8,000 land stations, 3,000 aircraft and 4,000 ships. In the developed countries, forecasting the atmospheric cycle of water for three days ahead has thus attained absolute precision in 80 per cent of cases. In the field of aviation alone this has enabled storms, fog and tempests to be avoided, thereby saving many human lives.

But these efforts of the WMO as yet cover only 20 per cent of the earth's surface. The underdeveloped countries—Africa, Asia and Latin America—through lack of means, and the oceans and reservoirs that are too vast to be covered by an organized network of observers, prevent a more accurate assessment and more trustworthy forecasting. From now until 1980 onwards, down to the year 2000, the programme now started off will weave, link by link, the net which is to cover the globe. And forecasting the behaviour of atmospheric moisture will, it is believed, improve from three to five and later to seven days. It will then be possible to work out the best routes for shipping, when and how to work, the best time and depth for sowing crops, where to spend a week's holiday in the sun . . . and perhaps, when the study of the cycle has reached this point, the raindrop may be harnessed so as to make it fall when and where we want it.

On its journey the drop of water sometimes takes up matter and sometimes gets rid of it; it either acts as a carrier or a depositor. When it rises from the ocean it is in the form of washed vapour; as it passes through the atmosphere it is augmented by human respiration and that of animals and plants, by natural gases and the exhaust from motor cars and aircraft; as it condenses into a cloud it is distilled like steam from warm water condensing in a cooled retort (when formed by an aircraft it is very pure and materializes into clouds at between 0°C. and −10°C.); as rain it contains oxygen and nitrogen in solution, sodium chloride in coastal areas, and, according to where it happens to be, magnesium, calcium, iodine, bromide, carbon dioxide, carbonates, ammonium nitrite, phosphates; and, when a storm is breaking, ozone. In passing through the soil it dissolves organic matter and carries nutritive elements which

The use of mineral waters has increased, now that water is so often polluted

Final checks before a meteorological satellite of the Tiros type is launched

Signs of underground water in the grotto of La Cave, in the Dordogne

Wells in the Sinai
Desert

Right: A water-point in the Hoggar

The Cayes region
in Haiti

it transfers on its way to men, animals and plants. If it accumulates in a pocket or finds a niche in a mineral deposit it may become a spring, mineral water or lime water, bicarbonated water, ferruginous water, as at Spa in Belgium, impregnated with sodium salts or radioactive.

Self-purification

Whether it be in lake, river or stream it encourages fermentation, stimulates bacterial growth and promotes its own purification . . . thus, the water which sustains us is clean—like a cat it is continually washing itself, and it keeps the world clean as well as getting rid of the waste. Its purity remains the guarantee of our very existence. One does not fish for one's life in troubled waters, and from this stems one of the dangers of the modern world, which has abused its waters, polluted them and is now suffering the consequences, from which it could perish unless steps are taken to redress the situation.

CHAPTER 4

THE DRINKING PROCESS IN ANIMALS AND IN VEGETABLE LIFE

With very few exceptions, according to C. Benezech, plants make their own food out of water and air. In order to live they behave like reciprocating pumps which suck up moisture from the soil, distribute it to their cells and release what is left over into the air. In fact, the system is one of double circulation. The roots collect the water which, with its contents of mineral food, rises up the stem to the leaves, where chlorophyll in the cells reacts with the water to produce glucose (or sugar), food for the plants, which descends again through a channel joined to the one by which it came up, while excess water is transpired through the stomata or pores of the leaves.

This continual upward and downward movement begins at the extremities of the root hairs which swarm in the soil, a buried network more complex than that of the underground sewage system of New York, Paris or London. A single plant of rye can carry 14 thousand million roots and radicles in a system totalling 400 miles in length. And the extremity of each of all the roots that the plant possesses carries innumerable hairs which multiply the absorbent surface 2,000 times. Every plant, capable of absorbing in this way up to 20 times its weight in water, induces consider-

able drainage of the soil up to 30 feet in depth (lucerne as much as 50 feet). Plants are perpetually thirsty.

But they return a proportion of their enormous absorption into the atmosphere through their leaves, in the form of dewdrops or water-vapour, through tiny pores known as stomata. A leaf can carry up to 325,000 stomata per square inch, mostly on its underside, allowing the entrance and exit of carbon dioxide and oxygen, elements essential for photosynthesis and growth. This transpiration, though inferior to the pumping action of the roots, nevertheless releases considerable quantities of water which, after this transmigration, rejoin the cycle from whence they came.

A field of lucerne, 2·5 acres in size, during its life transpires enough water to cover it to a depth of more than 24 inches; whereas the eucalyptus, a rare exception, consumes more than it gives out, and can thus be used to dry marshy land.

Process of osmosis

Water from the soil enters the rootlets of a plant by osmosis, a process which is found in almost all living tissues. It is by osmosis that molecules of water are enabled to tra-

The waterfalls at Iguazù, in Brazil

Fish in their natural habitat (far right, top)

Water-lilies in the Amazon basin (far right, below)

The famous "chandelier" in Underwood Park, California: 315 feet high, 20 feet across

Water in the middle of the village: Guadalupe in Spain

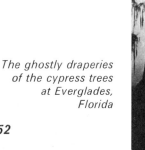

The ghostly draperies of the cypress trees at Everglades, Florida

verse living membranes which would appear to be impenetrable by its liquid drops and so reach the cells—cells that make up all living beings, whether single-celled or many-celled. Seen through the traditional microscope, these cells seem both transparent and homogeneous, but when the cells are viewed with an electron microscope and checked by the methods of modern biochemistry, they show an external plasmic membrane, and an inner nuclear membrane, linked by bridges to the former, and "recesses", the vacuoles, between the two membranes. These vacuoles are cavities filled with water and dissolved substances, substances which are absorbed or elaborated by the cell. Whether they like or dislike water, these vacuoles, which are recesses founded on water, swell or contract as they are filled with or emptied of water. A single cell plunged into clean water increases in volume at the same time as its vacuoles are filled and the inner pressure increases; but the same cell, plunged into salt or sugar solution, has its vacuoles diminished while their water escapes to the outside. If it is plunged into clear water once more, the cell's vacuoles will swell up again.

This series of changes, at present verified in the laboratory and found to take place in the cells of plants, animals and men, shows under the electron microscope that interchanges of water can and do take place constantly between the "recesses" and the exterior, and this movement of water and of the substances dissolved in it means that the continuity of living matter is assured. The phenomenon has been given the name of osmosis, the pressure developed is called osmotic pressure, and the whole process throws light on the fundamental rôle of water in life and, at the same time, on the particular way in which it passes through the plasmic membrane of the living cell.

The membrane of the cell, like all substances, is composed of molecules. And these molecules, although they are very close to one another, are nevertheless separated by spaces which have been well calculated: wide enough to allow molecules of water to pass through them, yet too narrow to allow this to happen quickly. So the drop of water, carrying the substances dissolved in it, passes through the barrier little by little—drop by drop, you might say.

This interchange, which plays a primary rôle in the passage of molecules through membranes and through all living tissues, is a logical result of the displacement of molecules. Like men on a crowded planet, they always tend to escape from a place where they are heavily concentrated to a place where they are scarcer. This can be seen when a lump of sugar is put into a cup of coffee, or a pinch of salt flavours a plate of leek soup, without the liquid having to be stirred round: the molecules of sugar or salt have simply spread themselves about.

The speed with which molecules pass through a membrane and its spaces, through osmosis, therefore involves all kinds of factors, such as the size of the molecules, the size of the spaces between the molecules, and the degree with which the molecules are concentrated on one hand or the other. Fine molecules, like those of water, pass much more easily through living membranes than the thicker molecules of mineral salts; and this difference in their ability to get through the membrane means that it plays a selective rôle, or, more precisely, that it acts as a filter, holding back the mineral substances and letting water through everything. Thus water carries

Icy torrent in the Oisans region of the Alps

The stubbornness of the sap in an agave, despite arid conditions

things, deposits them, passes on, loads itself and continues loaded, and in this way brings about the transfers and changes that mean first of all growth, and then life itself.

Mysteries remain

The way in which the membranes act as a filter, together with the movement of molecules, means that osmotic pressure is produced, and this plays a part, not just in the nutritional exchanges between a cell and what surrounds it, but in the spreading of the process all over the plant. The molecules of water,

The cactus's protection against transpiration (left)

Cascade on the Auvézère, in the Dordogne (right)

Landscape at Artibonite, Haiti (below, right)

Camels in the Gobi Desert, Mongolia (below)

which are at once more numerous and more concentrated on the outside of the plant than on its inner circuits, therefore pass from the part in which they are crowded to the part where they are less crowded. This current, or force, or pressure, is capable of making water rise several feet inside the veins of a tree.

Capillarity, which makes the hydrogen bridges of the molecule of water cling, one by one, to the oxygen of the molecule of water which it meets, also draws the nourishing water up the microscopic veins of plants, and so it keeps climbing up

Armour-plated lizard

way the plant begins to branch out from the very roots.

However, even considering all this, and adding together all the forces that act on it, there are still some things which remain un-explained—among them the size of the largest trees. But it is encouraging to think that there are still mysteries in nature and that water, which is present everywhere, is still not fully explained everywhere and in every way, for it is a proof of the element's vitality.

Circulation of water in animals is less puzzling: the heart, which acts as a suction and compression pump, helps capillarity and osmosis to feed the various parts of the body. But there, too, water stabilizes internal temperature, not only by modifying interior temperature changes through its latent heat, but also by regulating external temperature through sweating. It is indispensable for digestion as well as for purification. As in man, it removes waste by excretion. Some activities, such as breathing, perspiration or

Fruit trees irrigated by sprinkling in Haute-Garonne

them. But, in spite of all this, the way it climbs, at least in the giant trees, is not satisfactorily explained as yet. The transpiration of leaves also makes an empty space in the cells of their extremities, when the water has evaporated; this empti-ness attracts water in its place, be-cause nature hates any form of vacuum. The molecules of water are thus drawn upwards, all along the uninterrupted column, in spite of the

Irrigation by canals in Arizona: this has transformed the dry western lands into regions of model farming

Irrigation by rotative sprinkling in Florida

control of metabolic heat, so closely resemble the same functions in man that they will be dealt with later.[1]

For survival man must maintain a constant water equilibrium, but animals and plants, though unable to withstand indefinitely the dehydration produced by excessive heat or frost, can nevertheless exist between extremes which are as prodigious as they are varied.

[1] See Chapter 5: "Man and his Water."

The construction of the Aswan Dam, in Egypt: the material at the base being prepared, the water-passages being built, the sides and top of the dam being faced

Desert rodents live without drinking, eating only dry grasses, bark and dried fruits. A donkey can survive four days without drinking and lose 30 per cent of his weight, twice the loss which would kill a man. Moreover, the same donkey can recover by drinking 4 gallons of water in two minutes, a feat impossible for a man. The camel, whose sobriety is legendary, uses the fat from his hump, which can provide 9 gallons of water through oxidation.

Thus animals and plants cannot exist without water but, unlike man, they adapt easily to fluctuations in supply. The desert rodents which do not drink find their water partly in the seeds, grass and dry fruits, and to obtain the essential minimum they "manufacture" it, combining oxygen from the air with hydrogen from the seeds. Subsequently they provide a hydrated meal for pythons and boas or jackals and hyenas. The desert lizard is armoured with an impenetrable skin which impedes transpiration; it goes into hiding during the day and seeks its food at night, thus economizing on water in both cases. It is this adaptation to environment which is lacking in man; he creates the environment according to his requirements.

Plants are yet more adaptable.

Even if those of our temperate zone have to face up occasionally to a drought, they can interrupt or reduce their transpiration and at the same time their growth. The sentinel-cells of the stomata on the leaves do not keep their pores open unless they are full; if there is a shortage of water they shut the pores. Desert plants make use of the same system as the lizard; their stomata open only at night. Others, like the ocotillo, shed their leaves during drought and do not grow new ones until rain has fallen. The cactus has reduced its leaves to spines and grown a waxy skin which prevents the escape of any moisture. The echinocactus dilates its cylindrical body after rain and drinks from this reservoir, becoming deflated if the weather remains dry. Its white pulp, from which a drinkable liquid can be pressed, has saved many a lost traveller in the deserts of western America or the Brazilian drought areas. The tradescantia, whose seeds remain fertile for a very long time in dry conditions, grows with incredible speed at the first appearance of moisture. A shower of spring rain causes them to proliferate suddenly everywhere, then to disappear with equal suddenness.

Similar ingenuity is exhibited in the face of dehydration by freezing. The ice on a lake does not kill the plants around its margin nor the bacteria in its depths. Waters containing minerals are classified in three categories: "free" water which freezes at between $0°$ and $-6°C.$, capillary moisture, which only freezes at temperatures lower than $-6°C.$, and finally a "combined water" which does not solidify, even at $-20°C.$ Thus, pine trees can withstand up to $-40°C.$ in Siberia—and literature, to conjure up a picture of unimaginable cold,

Land brought into use in the province of Liberation, Egypt: the land has to be levelled, canals must be built and sluices provided, in order to raise ducks and grow oranges

tells tales of trees split by frost! Some organisms can survive after temperatures of $-252°$C.

Despite these extreme cases and exceptions it should not be forgotten that although an apple pip contains only 10 per cent of water, its fruit, when ripe, holds 80 per cent, a little more than a roast of beef (78·4 per cent) or a hen's egg (73·6 per cent), and that plants and animals, from the amoeba to the giant pine, all need water to exist and develop, especially man, to whom large quantities are vital.

In the Jura Vaudois, Switzerland, the consumption of water per acre of firs, pines and beeches has been measured, and this adds up for one year to 45 inches per acre for firs, 47 inches for pines and 44 inches for beeches; nearly

4 feet on every acre, 1,600 cubic yards or 270,000 gallons of water.

Wheat is much more greedy—between 60 and 120 inches of water on an acre for a single crop, or 320,000–670,000 gallons, according to the climate. How many gallons of water for a pound of bread?

The orange and the lemon are even more demanding—between 80 and 95 inches per acre, or from 450,000 to 530,000 gallons of water.

The cotton plant's needs are similar to those of the citrus fruits. Lucerne, which provides pasture for fattening cattle, exceeds this amount—from 131 to 145 inches per acre, between 730,000 and 810,000 gallons.

The quantity of water absorbed will obviously vary according to the climate. While the lucerne of our temperate regions consumes 710,000 gallons per acre, in Cyprus it needs up to 1,250,000 gallons.

In Cyprus, too, the banana demands 1,070,000 gallons, early tomatoes 450,000 gallons, maincrop tomatoes up to 600,000, while for autumn potatoes the requirement rises to 440,000. In the Egyptian Delta the rice crop needs 1,430,000 gallons per acre.

Praying for rain

This heavy consumption is influenced by climate and also by the time of year. Spring potatoes, like early tomatoes, are not so thirsty as autumn potatoes or maincrop tomatoes which grow during the hottest weather. The choice of

Land brought into use in the dry district of Brazil: water must be pumped from the São Francisco and pipes installed; then come the first crops — and neat plantations

varieties can therefore play an important part in water economy. But as yet few people bother about this; they are apathetic.

On the other hand, what has become quite clear to all concerned is the relationship between abundance of water and the size of the crop produced. Since ancient times farmers have known that without spring rain and the storms of June, July and August the year will be one of famine. For centuries prayers have been offered for water.

Modern statistics have proved this long recognized relation between rain and fertility. In the province of Konya in Turkey the rain which fell in 1928 helped to produce a crop of cereals which averaged 204 pounds per acre. In 1931 almost three times as much fell on Konya and the yield rose to an average of 1,400 pounds per acre.

Other statistics, still from Turkey but from the region of Diyarbakir, underline another fact of life which men have been aware of for a long time. It is not enough to have an adequate supply of rain; it must come at the right time. The same quantity of water fell on Diyarbakir in 1948 and 1949, but the crop for 1948 amounted to 100,000 tons, while that of 1949 fell to 34,000 tons. The rain fell at the wrong time.

If rain comes too early or too late, the plant undergoing its life-cycle will not find the necessary water for fruit-bearing or germination and will, according to the circumstances, either dry up or rot. How can the tap be turned on or off at will? Thus was the science of irrigation born.

In Iran the government appealed to the FAO[1] for help in the irrigation of new areas in the steppes of

[1] Food and Agricultural Organization, an agency of the United Nations.

Moghan. The perimeter irrigated will eventually be 75,000 acres, of which 15,000 are already settled, 18,000 ready to bring into cultivation and 42,000 ready to receive water.

In the Senegal basin, in Egypt, as a result of the Aswan dam, along the Mekong in Asia, in the loop of the São Francisco in Brazil—a recital of all the recent conquests of irrigation in famine-stricken countries needing quick results would be a very long one.

For irrigation, especially when associated with fertilizers, insecticides and fungicides, multiplies the yield. In the Middle East 21 per cent of the workable land is irrigated and this alone supplies 77 per cent of the total agricultural production.

Water consumption

But agriculturalists in the developed countries also take advantage of irrigation. Increasing or decreasing the supply of water can maintain production at its maximum level. To this end "supplementary irrigation" has been in operation for several years in Britain, covering an area of 100,000 acres, while in the state of New Jersey, U.S.A., although the average annual rainfall exceeds 40 inches, the amount of surface irrigation doubles every ten years and now stands at more than 125,000 acres. In France surface irrigation is in the neighbourhood of 2·5 million acres, but within the next twenty years there is likely to be double this amount. In Beauce the number of subterranean boreholes has multiplied, and on the Seine and its tributaries pumping stations have proliferated. The already enormous agricultural consumption of about 13 thousand million cubic yards a year, as against 5 thousand million for urban areas, is growing rapidly and sometimes doubles in less than five years.

Irrigation is a prolific consumer of water. The traditional type expends 5,300 cubic yards—890,000 gallons per acre a year. The yield increases, but half the water filters away and disappears. 2,200 gallons of water are necessary for producing 220 pounds of wheat, and 260 gallons are considered the bare minimum for sustaining life, a quantity capable of realizing a daily ration of 23 pounds of bread from the sowing of the grain to the baking process. If we add a pound of beef to this minimum, the requirement rises to 2,200 gallons a day; lucerne and cereals are thirsty, just like animals.

If we suppose that a few tomatoes and some fruit are also added to this meal, that irrigation uses up more and more water, and that the world population will double during the next thirty years, we begin to feel a twinge of anxiety.

Kandahar,
Afghanistan, entirely
irrigated

CHAPTER 5

MAN AND HIS WATER

An average man contains about 75 pints of water in his body, of which more than 5 pints are renewed every day. Water circulates in him as in an animal or plant, and man himself is a territory within the planetary cycle in which there exists another uninterrupted cycle which absorbs and rejects water. It is the same water, yet with a difference, which finds its way into him, travels within him, escapes and returns. In about twenty-odd days the same water no longer flows in him, though he still carries the same quantity. This water alternates from one point of the body to another in order to fulfil different purposes. The brain, the bones, the muscles, the kidneys and the blood all carry unequal amounts of water according to their function. Water, indispensable everywhere, is also beneficial in every sphere.

The human body does not draw all its water from the same source. Its origins are diverse, and only half is obtained by drinking. 40 per cent comes from foods which we imagine to be solid, ignoring the fact that meat and cheese themselves carry water too. The rest of the daily requirement is manufactured by the body by the combustion of food and tissues.

But aqueous circulation in the human body is not confined to the 5 pints which are renewed; about 14·5 pints a day are fed into the digestive system and reabsorbed by the mucous membranes, and there are 5·25 pints of intestinal juices, 2·5 pints of saliva and the same amount of gastric juices, 1·25 pints of pancreatic juice and 0·9 pint of bile. The movement is general and total; the blood and its circulation, the irrigation of cells, perspiration, respiration and excretion are all stages in the journey of a quantum of water which passes through the body and finally escapes in a daily amount equal to that absorbed, after playing its part in the vital processes.

There is no stagnant water in the body; every molecule of water in any part of the body at a given moment is somewhere else later, having been replaced by others. The greater part of these 75 pints is constantly recycled and re-used in passing from one function to another, sometimes transporting food, sometimes getting rid of waste products, but about 5 pints a day augments the cycle, which evacuates about 5 pints in compensation.

Nothing is lost, nothing is created; it is merely transformed. "Water," wrote C. Benezech, "is the structural and functional basis of living beings."

A powerful solvent, water breaks up the large fragments of food taken

The human body contains an average of 75 pints of water

Pastrana, in Spain

67

into the system and helps digestive hydrolysis. Without water there can be no digestion and consequently no processing of the large molecules which become the versatile, functional ingredients of living matter, nor can there be any of the metabolic reactions which accomplish the continuous destruction and reconstruction of the same living tissues, nor any regulation of temperature. In short, without water—nothing.

By working on the food it breaks up the large molecules (the molecular weight of which can be written in tens and hundreds of thousands); in particular, those of glucides (or carbohydrates) and protides (or albuminoids), in order to reduce them into compounds with smaller molecules—in particular into glucose and the small molecules of amino-acids which can then pass through the wall of the intestines, which cannot otherwise be breached. Without water, there would be no digestion—no absorption of food: the enzymes of the digestive juices only have to speed up the fundamental process in order to be of use.

Water thus breaks up the molecules within our tissues, but it also carries out an operation that is exactly the opposite: the making and synthesizing of the macromolecules that bring about a constant renewal of tissues and their functioning; these tissues are the basis of the body's energy. Inside the cells, these molecules, which have previously been made smaller, combine with the oxygen that is found in an aqueous solution (water again, without any other form), and make a series of metabolic reactions which keep destroying and rebuilding the tissues. This oxidation and burning up has a fundamental part to play, but the immediate and concrete

No trace of life in the Sahara Desert, south of Iharen

Water in a village of Chartreuse

Section of a kidney

results are divided into four parts: organic compositions that can be put into reserve (and in excess, these become obesity); heat; carbon dioxide, which the lungs exhale when we breathe out (moist breath, and so water again); and—still more water—the water used in the burning up of the food and tissues, which we have already examined, and which rounds off the whole synthesis.

Body heat balance

Perspiration, which must not be confused with transpiration, diffuses water-vapour through the skin invisibly and without being felt. Carried along by the blood-stream, which distributes it, the inner heat of the body is spread about in the surrounding air without leaving a trace, thus losing about 20 per cent of its own intensity.

Breathing also eliminates heat: in a relevant experiment, a muzzled dog was placed in a sweating-room at 43°C, and the animal's temperature went up 5°C in three-quarters of an hour. The same dog, in the same sweating-room, was allowed to pant, whereupon its temperature went up only 3°C in fourteen hours. In the same situation, a man would perspire. Perspiration only intervenes if the external temperature becomes too high, and it does so by

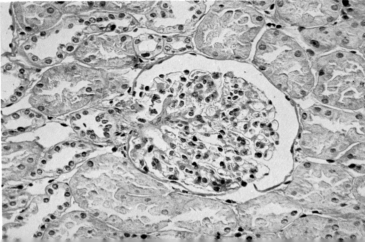

Construction of the dam at Entrepeñas in Spain

another means, the sudoriferous or sweat glands. The thermal equilibrium of man does not operate through the same channels when it is cold or when it is very hot, but it is always water which keeps it steady. It keeps it stable and at the same time controls all the internal chemistry of the body, maintaining it in good condition and guarding against sudden changes of pressure, acidity and composition.

Too much water or too little, in varying degrees, always harms a man. If he loses only 2 per cent of his normal total quantity, he immediately feels thirsty. If a man loses 5 or 6 per cent, his mouth and tongue dry up; if he loses under 10 per cent, his skin shrivels and he has hallucinations; a loss of less than 15 per cent means death! One of the characteristics of old age is a diminution in the percentage of water in the body. Man cannot live naturally in water; but he cannot live far from it, either.

Excess of water is also injurious, causing weakness and nausea. The medieval torture of forced ingurgi-

tation, even when applied only by degrees, led successively to mental confusion, loss of the sense of direction, trembling fits and ultimately coma and death.

Water, yes, but not too much or too little—both are fatal.

Control of quality, though less critical, is also important—the kidneys see to that. With the help of water, they filter and wash; and, besides this, they empty and regularize the body. Indeed, they achieve a regular balance, which we usually underestimate, between the food that varies every day and the body, the whole chemical and physical balance of which is maintained by the water that at the same time irrigates it, drains it, nourishes it and removes waste from it. Every day 350 pints of blood pass through the kidneys; and, through the almost universally solvent power of water, they concentrate, choose, reject and reabsorb, whilst freeing the body of about 3·5 cubic inches of waste every hour.

The excessive drinking of mineral waters, which are so popular today,

Dams influence the landscape. Here is the lake formed by the dam at Villefort, in Lozère

may be harmful. If they are taken merely as refreshment, and not for medical reasons—if they are carelessly chosen and over-mineralized —they may lead to stones in the bladder or haematuria, for which the only cure is often a surgical operation.

There are limitations to what the human kidneys can achieve; they cannot concentrate more than 2·2 per cent of salt in the urine, and this prevents man from drinking sea water, which contains 3·5 per cent. The bather who unintentionally swallows sea water dehydrates himself as he tries to eliminate the excess salt.

Sweat glands

Insensible perspiration eliminates 2 pints of water every day. Respiration also gets rid of 1 pint in exhaling carbon dioxide and breathing in the oxygen which is indispensable for life. Urinary excretion amounts to about 2 pints . . . and the 5 pints absorbed are accounted for.

In an equatorial desert when the sun is directly overhead, where the air is very dry and warm, the sweat secreted by the two million sweat glands in the body, two million miniature refrigerators, is itself capable of being as much as 17·5 pints under these extreme conditions. In a hostile environment such as the desert man is powerless to limit his consumption and elimination of water. On the other hand, he depends on an equivalent amount of absorption for his survival.

If these phenomena were better understood, many unprepared travellers would have avoided a painful death. If they had employed every possible means of reducing consumption and elimination of

water, such as keeping clothed, not moving during the day, keeping in the shade and remaining there until night, many would have survived. The rule is precise; about 5 pints are biologically necessary to man every day, and he replaces the exact equivalent when replenishing his stock. If he expends more under difficult circumstances he has to take in extra in order to maintain the fragile and vital equilibrium which will allow of no variation. About 5 pints of water per day per human being is the minimum consumption. But we have already seen that when bread, meat and fruit are added to the intake, millions of gallons of water are involved.

For washing, lighting, heating, clothing, transport or writing, water, water and still more water is indispensable. For washing and general purposes a man needs almost 10 gallons of water per day, 3,650 per annum. That is the consumption recorded in rural areas of the poorer countries. But with improvements in hygiene and the installation of modern sanitation the expenditure increases very rapidly, multiplying itself by five, ten or even more times. A shower-bath lasting five minutes uses 22 gallons of water, and a hair rinse 2·2 gallons a time. Washing the hands and face with soap and flannel consumes about 2·5 gallons but a daily bath multiplies this amount by ten. And how many times a day does a town-dweller wash his hands? Water which is on tap and does not have to be carried in buckets, drawn from a well or collected at a fountain, begins to flow faster and faster and in larger quantities. Thus it is that in a town the daily 10 gallons swell to about twenty-five gallons per person every twenty-four hours.

A lorry leaving the assembly line ready for the road, represents a

consumption of at least 45,000 gallons of water—37,000 in manufacturing the ton of steel in the vehicle and 8,000 in the process of assembly. More thousands of gallons have already been used in making the handles and knobs, glass and brakes. And the first gallon of fuel put into the tank will represent 80 gallons of water used in the refining process. What should we calculate for an aeroplane?

Let us visit a factory. There are offices surrounded by corridors off which are situated lavatories, washrooms and ice-water taps; workshops provided with the same amenities, except for the ice-water, but equipped with showers; taps in every corner of the building for cleaning the yards and workshops, transport, and for fire protection; also machines—thirsty machines.

A motor becomes hot as it works,

and to prevent it from seizing up it must be cooled with water. The condenser of a steam engine also needs cold water . . . how many millions or indeed tens of millions of machines are working in this way in the world, surrounded by water which is continually being renewed to cool them?

And this only applies to the general services common to all factories. Over and above this there are specialized uses; a freshly drawn, foaming pint of beer accounts for 44 pints of water according to I. Cheret.

Variety of uses

All the characteristics of water fit it for wide industrial use. Economical, pliable, adaptable and easy to handle, its facile temperament is augmented by its qualities as a solvent, its important coefficient of heat exchange and its density, all attributes which are conferred on it by its combination of two hydrogen atoms with one of oxygen.

It has an infinite variety of uses corresponding with its nature. The 44 pints which went into the making of 1 pint of beer first watered the barley from which the malt was extracted, then converted it into mash and brewed it.

For slaughtering and processing a calf or a sheep a minimum of 110 gallons is required. A dairy needs 4 pints of water to supply a pint of milk and between 5 and 10 pints for a pound of butter. In paper-making 25 gallons have to be added before a pound of the end-product can leave the machines.

Here it is essentially the solvent qualities of water which are being employed. In another sphere 1·5 gallons, with the addition of a detergent, have to be used for washing a pound of wool.

But water is not only a solvent. In the metallurgical industry 3,400 gallons of water are consumed for every ton of steel—about 820 gallons in the blast furnace, 500 gallons in the coke ovens, 600 in the main shop, 600 in the rolling mills, 45 in the boilers and 835 gallons shared among various other installations. At this level water has become a primary material; in the production of 300,000 tons of steel, the 1 million tons of iron and the 350,000 tons of coke are no more important than the indispensable 45 million tons of water.

To clothe a man, 65 gallons of water are needed to turn washed wool into a pound of cloth.

For housing we can start by calculating 38 gallons of water as being expended before a hundredweight of cement can be produced.

Surely the basic necessities of life are covered by all this; washed, fed, clothed and housed, the average man seems to be amply provided for.

Indeed he is not; he still needs electricity.

In the U.S.A. the large hydro-electric schemes like the one at Niagara Falls supply about two hundred and fifty million million kilowatt-hours of electric power out of the country's total. There, as in other places, it would be difficult to see clearly without the help of water, for in order to achieve this result 4,000 million million gallons have to be used.

The thermal and nuclear power stations which complete the production network in the United States use water, like the rest of the world, in this case for cooling. In a typical thermal plant the amount expended is in the neighbourhood of 2,000 gallons per second. In terms of water, what does the reading of this book in a well-lighted armchair in the evening represent?

The nuclear power station at Chinon, Indre-et-Loire

A nuclear plant of the same capacity—for example, that at Chinon—demands over 4,000 gallons, nearly double for the same task. It is understood that from now on the large nuclear power stations of the future are to be built beside the sea. There a mere handful of rivers will be able to do the job. The Seine, with a flow of almost 8,000 gallons per second, would be pumped dry by a 500 megawatt nuclear power station.

Water consumption

Our typical man, now housed, clothed and provided with lighting, still uses up water without knowing it. If the petrol which he uses or the sand mixed with the cement for his house has travelled by barge on the canals, more water has been consumed by evaporation and spillage. The canals of the north of France alone lose 210 million cubic yards a year by evaporation and seepage.

The average inhabitant of New York uses over 130 gallons of water a day not counting that consumed by his food and his industrial needs; the whole of French industry gets through over 15 thousand million cubic yards a year as against 5 thousand million for the needs of urban communities and 13 thousand million for agricultural purposes.

Man demands more water every day for bodily hygiene and food; he is using increasing amounts in industry and agriculture, he congregates in towns, and the demand for water grows on all sides, doubling and trebling, while at the same time the population figures rise.

Nevertheless the margin would be sufficiently large—in France, for example, where consumption is of the order of 34 thousand million cubic yards as against resources in rivers, streams and lakes of 220 thousand million cubic yards—if these resources contained unpolluted water.

Thus it is that, in our own age, after the struggles against water and then the struggles with water, the struggle to find more water is beginning.

CHAPTER 6

THE WAY WATER
IS OVERLOADED

Water is soft and never still, and together with its ability to dissolve matter, this means that one of its characteristics is the power to swallow up waste matter, break it up, and finally change it into substances that are either useful or else diluted until they are harmless; for instance, when there is too much magnesium in water, it is a laxative, but when magnesium is there in very small doses it is beneficial, because it becomes part of the composition of the bones, and a total lack of it may lead to cancer. Water purifies itself and at the same time nourishes itself.

As it moves, water shakes up waste matter, dissolving some of it and breaking up the rest. The water of a river or a lake that has begun its work by breaking up waste and beginning to dissolve it, can continue to press on with the good work; it has absorbed oxygen from the air, and taken in oxygen put out by the aquatic plants during photosynthesis; thus, doubly reinforced and remarkably vigorous, it sets about metabolizing the waste matter, just as happens in the tissues of a living organism. There, too, it oxidizes them—"burns" them up— and the combustion of organic waste leaves nothing but water, carbon dioxide and some light cinders. At the same time, the water will distribute the oxygen it has taken in to innumer-able active bacteria which feed on organic waste and used waters, making useful substances out of them which the movement of the water then carries away, spreads, disperses and deposits on its banks and beds.

Apart from bacteria, water is populated by hundreds of thousands of microscopic creatures such as diatoms, unicellular brown-coloured algae, whose dead bodies form important deposits in lakes and act as food for fish. Here, too, the oxygen in the water is a very important factor, as in all the processes which take place in water for transforming carbon dioxide into the organic carbon of living matter.

Water, this remarkable vehicle for purification and regeneration, modestly requires only oxygen to nourish all these activities with their many causes and effects.

"Indigestion"

But if a quantity of water is overloaded with waste matter it exhausts itself in the process of elimination, using up all its oxygen. This, in fact, is a form of "indigestion", and the water can no longer either purify or regenerate. A new infusion of oxygen will be necessary to bring back its power to feed, and if the waste matter does not allow

Fishing on the banks of the Seine

it breathing space, accumulates too quickly and proliferates, it becomes less and less able to fulfil its task and more and more polluted.

The colour of water gives a clue as to its pollution. Solar radiation is absorbed by pure water, but the absorption varies according to the wavelength of the light. It is the shorter wavelengths, those in the vicinity of blue, which are least absorbed, and for this reason pure water looks blue if it is deep enough. The green, yellow or brown colour of some water is merely produced by alteration of the medium, either physical, due to matter in suspension, or chemical, due to such factors as the existence in solution of substances from the surrounding soil.

But, as R. Colas insists, the degree to which a river or a lake is polluted must be determined more scientifically than this: merely looking at it is not enough. In addition to elements such as calcium, iodine, fluorine, lead and copper, among others, as well as arsenic and chromium, water can also carry typhus and dysentery, cholera and poliomyelitis; in short, water must be analysed in order that its degree of pollution may be established, and its turbidity and its colour must be examined for traces of nitrates, lead or sulphates by passing it through radioactive substances. In order to avoid this long series of examinations, two measures are generally taken first: the BOD (biochemical oxygen demand) and the COD (chemical oxygen demand). The former measures organic pollution by measuring the quantity of oxygen necessary to dissolve waste; but it cannot measure inorganic pollution, such as industrial waste, for instance. It is the COD, or chemical oxygen demand, which measures inorganic pollution by saturating the substances present in the water with an oxidizing agent, permanganate of potassium.

But it is debatable whether the COD can really measure whether water is drinkable. Not because it is an inexact or inadequate measurement, but because the variety of forms in which pollution occurs creates a situation which has complex and unforeseeable biological consequences. In fact, the combined presence in water of chemical substances of various types, even when the concentration of each is only minimal, can produce a cumulative toxic effect, a multiplication of danger which will not be revealed by analysis.

In the end we have to thank the "test-fish" for revealing the degree of toxicity of a particular water. Barred cages containing fishes are, for example, immersed at 50 yards above and below the outflows of a factory and observed at regular intervals. If the effluents are toxic the fish which are downstream perish while the others remain unharmed. The "test-fish" is man's only way of obtaining the necessary information.

Excess of oxygen

Every time a quantity of water is obliged to consume too much oxygen in proportion to the amount it contains, it falls sick. Anglers are the first to find this out. This excessive consumption of oxygen is the result of overloading, which can happen in many ways. The addition of nutritive elements, for example, will, like a fertilizer, promote the selective growth of plankton, diatoms or algae, to the detriment of some other forms of life. Their proliferation, absorbing oxygen, reduces the proportion available elsewhere, and certain species of fish, hitherto flourishing, fall ill and disappear, to the benefit of other species which use less oxygen and have a different way of life. As the effects increase these species disappear in their turn and asphyxia leads to final extinction. The oxygen dissipates in the exhausted water and the majority of the living organisms which it normally carries eventually vanish.

This is what happens in dead waters crammed with nitrates and phosphates, polluted by industry and agricultural fertilizers dissolved by running streams which carry the pollution to lakes, rivers and even to the sea.

Opposite New York, in the area of urban and industrial pollution, 20 square miles of the ocean have been christened "The Dead Sea"!

Warning from anglers

The anglers must be listened to and heeded. It is they who forewarn us. Their complaints are the most serious of the alarm signals, for they are the best observers of "test-fish".

What are they complaining about? In France at Toul it is about a factory making plastics which discharges ammonium salts, chlorides and phenols into the river. The water is covered with oil-slicks and foam. At Mazamet the complaint concerns the wool industry, which discharges water contaminated with grease into the Arnette. In the north it is the sugar factories which inundate the canals with effluents. At Tartas, in the south-west, paper-mills pollute the Adour. In the east, during the month of May, 1963, according to an angling magazine, one laboratory alone investigated, after complaints by anglers, nine cases of pollution by dairy-produce manufacturers, eight by urban

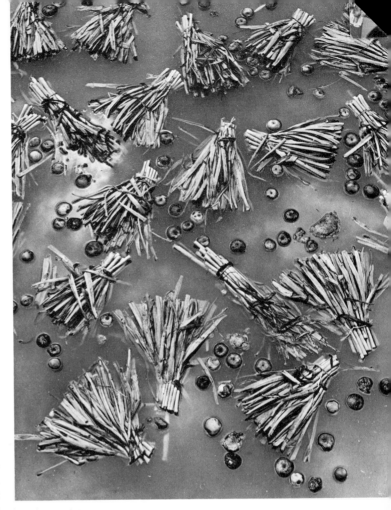

Vegetables and fruit thrown into drains at Avignon

"Test fish" in a river in the United States. Those corpses might just as well be found in France, Britain, Germany or Italy

Domestic water

Factories pour waste of all kinds into the rivers

sewage, three by slaughterhouses and canneries, three by metallurgical industries, two by chemical industries, four of miscellaneous origin and one just classed as "mysterious".

Similar cries of anger are heard on the banks of the Rhine, in Italy, Britain and the United States. Pollution threatens. Or rather, a number of varieties of pollution threaten, for the anglers tell us that the cases of contamination are both fluctuating and diverse. There is a general asphyxiation of water, but from a multiplicity of pollutions.

Pollution is one of the results of population growth. So long as the population was small and scattered natural purification took care of the cleaning process. But the more the density of the population increases the greater the degree of contamination becomes, reaching levels where

it multiplies each type of dirt, aggravating the others. Sociologists and hydrologists have christened this modern phenomenon "collective" pollution. It is identical, for example, with the case of mud stirred up in canals or rivers, harmless enough so long as the movement of the water is not too agitated by the passage of power-driven boats, so that the disturbance of the mud spoils the equilibrium of aquatic life, clogs the water, interferes with the process of oxygenation and turns the flow of clear water into a muddy stream.

The Parisian conurbation will soon contain 10 million inhabitants. It is to be hoped that its waste water will all be biologically treated in the near future. The quantity of residual sludge will then reach a total of 13,000 cubic yards every day, con-

Above: Pulpwood arriving at the paper-mills.
Right, above: An example of progress: in Dakar, this canal, which is to carry away rain water, is also used to remove household waste. Right, below: Fishing in the favellas of Rio de Janeiro

taining 600 tons of dry matter three or four complete train-loads every twenty-four hours will be needed to get rid of it. And to get rid of where? It is difficult to imagine the stockpiling of a daily quantity of these proportions without provoking a new imbalance somewhere else—another piece of pollution.

Waste disposal

Household waste is also a form of collective pollution. Every inhabitant of New York produces over 5 pounds of it per day, and the people of Europe are beginning to approach this figure too. In town and country, in London or in Florence, in France or in Germany, this refuse is sometimes burned, sometimes buried, but often it is piled up in containers in the open air to be watered by the rain. This washing process carried out continuously in a model refuse depot of reduced scale, 12 yards long by 10 wide and 10 deep, extracted in less than a year 3·3 tons of bicarbonate, 1·5 tons of sodium and potassium, 1 ton of calcium and magnesium, 0·31 ton of chloride and 0·23 ton of sulphate. All these mineral salts accumulating in close proximity to one another in underground waters seriously upset the balance.

Thus underground water sources, which are increasingly sought after, are being seriously polluted before they have even been used.

Pollution of underground water by hydrocarbons, especially liquid derivatives of petroleum—petrol, benzene, paraffin, oils, tars, gas-oil and fuel-oil—is also very insidious, extremely widespread, little-recognized and rapid.

All eyes are focused on oil-tankers which, after each trip, clean out their tanks at sea and empty 3 or 4 million tons of water contaminated with petroleum into the oceans of the world. The great oil centres in which refineries and chemical works are grouped in coastal areas possess the same injurious powers. From the Bay of Bahia in Brazil to that of Berre in France these serious cases of pollution are found.

But until recently this pollution, which paints thin, glistening films of oil on the sea, had not reached the proximity of domestic water supplies. For a few years this has no longer been the case. It has become more economical to site refineries near centres of consumption inland, feeding them from the ports by means of pipelines. These pipelines wind their way through the soil, through subterranean water sources and across rivers . . . and despite all precautions leakages

have occurred. Any river or lake involved becomes completely contaminated. The refinery itself, from the start, through its exhalation of petroleum gases and its leakages, contaminates its environment, especially the water which it uses, the river which runs beside it and the underground water in the vicinity. And this in spite of the strictest precautions.

In a less spectacular fashion every petrol-pump which loses some petrol each day, every fuel tank which supplies the central heating system of a house or the power unit of a factory is a source of pollution. Well-authenticated estimates affirm that 1 gallon of petrol can contaminate between 6,000 and 30,000 cubic yards of water, or from 1 million to 5 million gallons. A small 4 gallon drum of motor fuel could pollute the daily consumption of a town of 200,000 inhabitants. A single tanker lorry of 3,000 gallons capacity would pollute the consumption of the same town for a period of two years.

In Germany it has been calculated that over 300 cubic yards of petrol and fuel oil have infiltrated into underground water supplies, rendering over 300 million cubic yards unfit for consumption—5 per cent of the total requirement.

Hydrologists protest against the contamination arising from hydrocarbons; doctors, too, rise in revolt. Out of 60 derivatives of petroleum, 40 change the taste of water, 24 are toxic and certain of them are suspected of causing cancer.

Man-made detergents

Synthetic detergents, though a modern invention, succeed nevertheless in inflicting a threefold type of pollution on the water which contains them. Introduced about fifteen years ago, these new aids to

housekeeping and industry are used for cleaning and maintenance in the home and in the factory.

They are also employed in the metallurgical and the petroleum industries, for the preparation of insecticides, fungicides, herbicides, pharmaceutical products and cosmetics. And they persist in water after use, manifesting their presence by foam, not only in the washbasins but in the neighbourhood of dams and locks. They form about 15 per cent of washing powders.

Hong Kong: domestic chores of inhabitants who live on the water

Some of the rubbish that soon piles up in a large city during a dustmen's strike in Paris

In the bay of Bahia, where derricks are employed for oil-drilling under the sea, and the oil is carried by pipeline to the land

Synthetic detergents fall into three categories, and the first of these, that of ammoniac detergents, has been progressively banned from use in all the developed countries. Their scum accumulates against dams and locks to an extent which makes navigation dangerous. The cationic detergents, also dangerous, have practically gone out of use. The detergents called biological, which are more easily destroyed by micro-organisms, are being used to a greater extent.

The scum has disappeared from washing machines and from rivers. Ingenious advertising campaigns, after trumpeting the virtues of foaming water, now maintain that latherless water is much more effective, and biological detergents have replaced the ammoniac ones.

Pollution is aggravated by their presence, not only as a supplementary contaminant but as an obstacle to reoxygenation of the water. A little more detergent always means a little more dead water. In purification plants the same detergents hamper and alter the biological activity of the bacteria, and the water preserves traces of their existence even after treatment. And they carry this taint, slight but persistent, which affects the water we drink and the water used for washing the vegetables which we eat. Too rapid rinsing of a receptacle washed in detergent, in restaurant or home, will add to that dose which eventually reaches proportions detrimental to health through the successive accumulation of small quantities.

In fact, recent studies have raised a number of questions, apart from aggravated contamination of water, as to the chronic toxicity arising from man's intake of extremely small but significant doses of detergent. They facilitate absorption by the intestines of a multitude of

At the end of the bay of Bahia—the
refinery and its stores. When oil is
drilled for, even tiny leaks, added
together, make fishing more and more
difficult

The snowy foam of detergents, in France (above) and in the United States (right)

harmful substances, and some researchers have even advanced the theory that the cancerous action of certain chemical additives is stimulated by them.

Experiments have shown that absorption by mice of certain hydrocarbons in the presence of detergents significantly accelerates the formation of cancer of the stomach. The same proof has been furnished by 3–4 benzpyrene, a well-known cancer-forming hydrocarbon which, when administered to laboratory animals in weak doses over a period of 400 days, produced cancerous growths only in the presence of detergents dissolved in the drinking water.

Use of chemical fertilizers and synthetic pesticides in agriculture has soared prodigiously since the end of World War II. Since their massive employment generates an increase in yield and a reduction in labour, all the factors have combined to produce excessive infiltration.

If fertilizers are to be of maximum efficiency, their phosphates must be totally soluble. The result of this is that mineral fertilizers rich in phosphorus compounds and nitrates rapidly introduce into rivers, either through the flow or by invading underground water sources, a degree of indirect pollution resulting from the salts and direct pollution from the toxic compositions which arise from this.

"Blue sickness"

We have already observed how an excess of nutritive salts stimulates the proliferation of algae and, by a chain reaction, causes the death of the water. This is indirect pollution.

Direct pollution is like this. An acre of cultivated land impregnates the water which passes through it with a little less than a pound of nitrogen a year. Now it has been shown that increased use of nitrogenous fertilizers leads to greater enrichment of this water. The presence of nitrates, even in minimal quantities, produces the "blue sickness" in aquatic life. This same nitrogen in contact with river bottoms and lake beds and with fermenting organic matter runs the risk of creating an excess of nitrates. Aquatic life is incompatible with its presence. It is for this reason that nitrates are banned as fertilizers in the ricefields of Japan.

The production of synthetic insecticides exceeded 400,000 tons in 1967, of which three-quarters comprised organo-chlorides,[1] among them the amazing DDT, of which, according to the previous year's estimate, more than 1,600,000 tons had already been spread on the cultivated soils of the world.

In this case it was the hunters who first sounded the alarm. Anglers had not yet done so, having generally seen no connection between the depopulation of a river and the tractor or aircraft spraying pesticide a few miles away. Hunters, however, had connected the disappearance of pheasants, partridge and quail with the invasion of pesticides.

Today all the waters of the world are contaminated by residues of organo-chloride pesticides like DDT, which in ten years loses only 50 per cent of its original mass. Systematic research in rivers and streams, lakes, and among the inhabitants of ocean depths and even the eternal snows, in places far removed from all human activity, has revealed general contamination, sometimes in minute quantities, sometimes in significant doses. Even in the Antarctic the water is lightly tainted. DDT has been discovered in the tissues of fish at Ross Island, in seal-blubber from the Weddell Sea and in the fat of penguins in Adélie Land.

The chemical factories which make these pesticides discharge industrial effluent into rivers, interfering with the hydrologic cycle. Dissemination over a large surface area, by tractor or by aircraft, aggravates the contamination which rain spreads across the surface or infiltrates deep into the ground. In this way lemons in Mississippi were found to contain a chemical preparation sold for destroying a caterpillar injurious to sugar-cane. Campaigns

---

[1] A synthetic insecticide containing a minimum of three atoms of chlorine in its molecule.

for exterminating mosquitoes provide an example of factors which spread pollution. Furthermore, up to 50 per cent of the dosage of organo-chloride volatilizes into the atmosphere, is carried by the wind, borne on atmospheric currents, dispersed on a vast scale and returned to earth or sea by precipitation. And all our waters are infested.

DDD, for example, a close relative of DDT, renders birds sterile; what effect could it have on man?

Many thermal waters such as medicinal muds possess a certain amount of natural radioactivity due to the presence of the radioactive elements radium and thorium. At this dose-rate the radioactivity is beneficial.

But industry and nuclear research laboratories nowadays prepare thousands of artificial radioactive elements, and their manufacture inevitably contaminates water or releases quantities of effluent.

But apart from this, every year a nuclear plant accumulates several pounds of fission products which need to be eliminated. These radioactive residues are treated so as to concentrate the maximum amount of radioactivity in the smallest possible space, which gives rise to two categories of atomic waste: solid and liquid residues of powerful activity to be carefully packaged and stored, and liquid effluents of weak radioactivity which it is possible to discharge into rivers and streams provided that the correct security precautions are carried out.

In 1958 the intensely radioactive

In order that fertilizers may be spread, they are mixed with the water used for irrigation, and so cause direct pollution

residues produced in the world already amounted to 10,000 tons. In 1965 they exceeded 100,000 tons. A total of 10,000,000 tons is forecast for the year 2000.

It is also forecast for the year 2000, so far as slightly radioactive liquid effluents are concerned, that there will be 60 thousand million curies in more than a million and a quarter cubic yards of water.[1]

The nightmare results which an excess of radioactivity can cause are now only too well-known, so that a large number of precautions are being taken against this form of pollution.

Thermal pollution

Recent, still novel, little understood and undetected by classical methods of analysis, thermal pollution, without provoking complaint, conquers territory which it never occupies. It passes across it wantonly and changes it for the worse.

All the motors in the world, all the nuclear installations on earth, all the factories on this planet, use water for cooling, and this warms it up. The cooling water of a thermal power station, for example, is returned to the river whence it came without apparently undergoing the slightest pollution. Chemical analysis reveals no alteration. Nevertheless, the heat which it has absorbed is not dissipated until it has flowed about six miles. And for the whole of that distance the heat of the water will have given rise to a decrease in oxygen content and because of this will have affected the fauna and flora of the river. When the United States foresee that in their country in 1980 a sixth of

[1] The figure for 1970 was 3 thousand million curies in 35,000 cubic yards of water.

the surface waters and in 2000 a third will be used for cooling ther-

[handwritten annotations: 13° to 26°C = 13°/° — oxygen / consumption of O increases / evaporation / no foreing matter — less of oxygen. / die from variations of temperatures.]

...ations ...or the ...ations ...rstood ...n will ...of the ...r rises ...entra-...n of oxygen diminishes by 13 per ...nces, ...the ...mical ...se are ...ation, ...n in-...antity ...ater is ...n can arise from this, an accumulation of unassimilated waste and partially oxidized organic matter, while at the same time evaporation increases. Unlike other forms of pollution, no foreign matter is involved. All that has happened is that the water has lost part of its most active constituent—oxygen.

We can, if we like, consider that we live in a world which is too fragile or too delicately balanced, seeing that it will not tolerate without detriment a few degrees increase in temperature, but this is a fact. The oysters of Chesapeake Bay in Maryland and Oyster Creek Bay in Florida died from variations of temperature. Such variations can have the effect of killing certain species while benefiting others, thus disturbing the balance of Nature, with unpredictable results.

We cannot really tell. Thermal pollution is too recent for all its dangers to be recognized. Nor do we yet know the precise range of temperatures within which the major species of fish and aquatic organisms can survive.

We only know the grave nature of this new type of pollution. Two American scientists have calculated that certain rivers in the United States whose waters are particularly in demand for cooling purposes would begin to boil in 1985 and would be completely dried up by 2010 unless stringent preventive measures were taken.

Dying rivers

In short, man, born from water, brought up by it and nourished by it, has abused it to such an extent that he can no longer rely on it.

Weighted down by the successive burdens of drinking, agriculture, industrialization, cleaning, the cycle regeneration, loaded besides with harmful substances, sediments, filth and effluents, water is stealing away. Sometimes it dies. For example, within a few days this year French newspapers announced: "A river flowing into the English Channel, the Douve, and its tributary the Merderet, are carrying some thousands of dead fish, especially pike and bream." "A leak in a fuel-oil tank at Vilatte de Vienne (Isère) polluted the river Sevenne for 7 kilometres, as fas as its confluence with the Rhône. The fauna and flora were entirely destroyed." "The Marne is polluted over several kilometres between Boulogne and Joinville (Haute-Marne). Fish have died in their thousands and the whole of the aquatic fauna in the sector has been destroyed. The cause of the contamination is unknown." "The Iton is polluted for several kilometres below Evreux. Thousands of fish have succumbed and a fish-breeding project partially destroyed. An inquiry has established that the river was polluted by acid discharged from an outfall at Evreux." "For some days the Sarthe, like the Rhine

a month ago, has borne many traces of fuel oil, and probably also of toxic disinfec̲ts, since the water is grey. T̲ of dead fish float on the s̲ a nauseating smell per-v̲ atmosphere around M̲ne." "In the Auzon, ne̲-les-Mines (Puy de Dô̲ have been killed over a 2̲ stretch by a dangerous pes̲ for spraying apple tree̲nual General Assembly̲ industrialists of the Mid̲ concerned about the pollution of the Vienne by paper mills on its banks." "The Bèche (Puy de Dôme), though only a little stream in the mountains, has had its water contaminated by effluent from the Superbasse power station." "For several days the Orne has been poisoned below the town of Argentan. On this occasion the Departmental Committee for Social and Sanitary Action draws the attention of the public to the danger of bathing in this river and of eating any fish which may have been caught in it."

We cite these extracts word for word, without comment.

The water of Paris and the region around it, emanating chiefly from the Seine and the Marne, is discharged back into the Seine after only partial purification. And it is now a commonplace saying in summer when the water is low that from Clichy downwards a double mixture flows in the Seine, half water and half sewage. In the middle of Paris on very hot days the flow of the Seine drops to a few cubic yards per second, and the water, exposed for a long time to the sun, becomes completely unsuitable for fish to live in, owing to its temperature and its low oxygen content.

In Switzerland lakes are dying. The slow death of the Lake of Morat is the most spectacular. Proliferation of the alga *Oscillatoria rubes-*

cens, has given it a red colour which popular legend attributes to the blood of Burgundians who fell there in ancient times.

Lake Constance, which supplies drinking water to certain parts of Switzerland and Germany, collects in good years and bad years alike about 85 million cubic yards of heavily impregnated water which arrives from the urban centres and factories of Switzerland, Austria and Germany. Algae are breeding in

it with a vigour which is causing increased anxiety. An agreement signed in 1969 between Switzerland, Austria and Germany should enable it to lead a more oxygenated existence.

The Lake of Geneva itself—in spite of its size and depth, its surface area of 224 square miles and its bottom at 985 feet, which should allow organic deposits to turn into mineral matter before reaching the bed—this lake, too, begins to show signs of fatigue. Its state of health is not going well. On the one hand the transparency of its waters and the amount of oxygen in its lower levels is decreasing progressively; on the other hand its content of ammoniacal nitrogen, nitrites and phosphates shows a massive increase, as does its bacteriological pollution.

World-wide pollution

The Rhine, an international waterway becomes increasingly polluted as it winds its way towards Holland. The waste waters of the cities it passes, including Strasbourg and Cologne, the deposits of mining operations, salt works, chemical industries and the heavily laden waters of the Ruhr rivers, combine to produce this result: 2,000 germs per square yard above Strasbourg, 1,500,000 at its mouth. Amsterdam in August 1969 had only one week's reserve of drinking water.

In Belgium the Meuse, after it has left Liège to enter the industrial region of Dutch Limburg, shows disquieting signs of deterioration in its waters.

In England the pollution of estuaries and the rivers which flow into them attains levels among the highest in the world under the triple burden of urban concentration, mining and intensive industry. Pollution there is often of exceptional gravity.

Germany possesses a typical example of a polluted region in the Ruhr, but all the waterways are controlled by a number of organizations with dictatorial powers which possess the authority to cure the trouble.

In the U.S.S.R., despite the abundance of waters and the extent of the territory, the situation is as difficult as in Western Europe. 225,000 miles of rivers are already classed as polluted and the damage done to

Towns prepare to clean their water. First it is decanted, which removes floating material, and then it is aerated through small stones. Subsequently, after being passed through a "digester" of mud, it is filtered through a bacterial layer. Purification plant at Corbeil-Essonnes.

Waste spread in drying tanks covered in snow (above and right)

In the eastern states pollution has become so intense that its gravity has given rise to severe legislation and the imposition of penal sanctions and fines on offenders. The Nixon administration has stepped up preventive and suppressive measures. Student organizations have mounted an anti-pollution crusade which has received impressive support from all quarters.

Large lakes, to take just this one blatant example, have been and still are the special battleground of this gangrene, where pollution can be seen at its worst.

Clear Lake, 94 miles from San Francisco, in the mountains, is a lake well stocked with fish, but at the same time it is the chosen preserve of a relative of the mosquito, *Chaeoborus astictopus*. It is not a bloodsucker, but it stings, and it is obstinate, extremely prolific and audacious. In 1949 an attack of great intensity was mounted on it after meticulous preparation. The volume of the lake was calculated, the surface reconnoitred and laboratory trials initiated. The chosen insecticide was DDD, which appeared to be less harmful to the fish, and it was applied in such a way that its concentration could not exceed one part in 70 million parts of water.

The mosquitoes were decimated but they were not eliminated completely. In 1954, to finish off this source of irritation, a new onslaught was launched. This time the proportion of poison was raised to one part in 50 million parts of water. Like Carthage, the mosquitoes had to be destroyed at all costs. In the following winter more than a hundred grebes—web-footed birds with rudimentary wings and pearly ventral plumage—were found dead. The grebe settles on the margins of Clear Lake, as on those of the lakes of Savoie, to nest and to feed on the

fisheries alone already amounts to more than 200,000 dollars. The river Donetz in the heavily industrialized region of the Don basin receives, it is said, over a million cubic yards of water polluted by sugar refineries, steel plants and mining operations. Pollution is an evil which is spreading fear.

The U.S.A., by the vastness of its industrial activity and its concentration, the size of its cities and their way of life, exceeds all other nations in the scale of its pollution— the ransom of success. Contamination by detergents, pesticides and hydrocarbons mingles with pollution by household waste and the collective and thermal types, growing and multiplying.

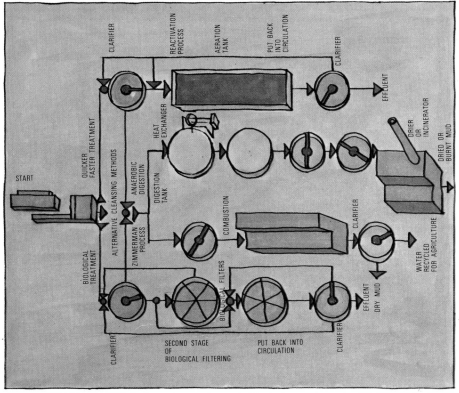

START

QUICKER FASTER TREATMENT

CLARIFIER

REACTIVATION PROCESS

AERATION TANK

PUT BACK INTO CIRCULATION

CLARIFIER

EFFLUENT

ALTERNATIVE CLEANSING METHODS

HEAT EXCHANGER

ANAEROBIC DIGESTION

DIGESTION TANK

DRIER OR INCINERATOR

DRIED OR BURNT MUD

BIOLOGICAL TREATMENT

ZIMMERMAN PROCESS

COMBUSTION

CLARIFIER

WATER RECYCLED FOR AGRICULTURE

CLARIFIER

BIOLOGICAL FILTERS

EFFLUENT DRY MUD

CLARIFIER

SECOND STAGE OF BIOLOGICAL FILTERING

PUT BACK INTO CIRCULATION

Complete circuit of water, constantly purified

abundance of fish during the winter.

In 1954 the obstinate mosquito was still on the rampage. The lake was given a third dose of treatment; more grebes died. Analysis of their fatty tissue revealed an amazing concentration of DDD, 1,600 parts per million. How was this possible when the maximum dose applied to the water had been 1 part to 50 millions? Analysis was then carried out on the inhabitants of the water; the plankton contained 5 parts per million, fish feeding on aquatic plants 40 to 300 parts per million, and fish feeding on other fish, like the bull-head, 2,500 parts per million. The poison had been absorbed by the lower organisms and concentrated, subsequently passing from organism to organism, accumulating more at each step.

Worse, in 1959, two years after the last treatment with DDD, the plankton still contained 5·3 parts per million of the poison, which had long since disappeared from the water itself. Fish hatched nine months after the treatment were also contaminated, and Californian grebes and gulls carried 2,000 parts per million of poison. The mosquitoes are still biting but the grebes have almost disappeared; there were only 60 survivors in 1960 out of an original count of 2,000, and those 60 were sterile.

What will happen to the man who feeds on fish or fowl contaminated by DDD and who becomes contaminated himself in turn? DDD destroys that part of the suprarenal glands which constitutes the adrenal cortex, secreter of hormones. Deficiency of adrenalin in the blood produces depression, hypotension, absence of vasco-constriction . . . an extremely heavy price to pay for polluting water in the hope of getting rid of swarms of troublesome mosquitoes.

The complex of great lakes in North America—Erie, Ontario, Superior, Huron and Michigan, which lie on the boundary of the United States and Canada, and on whose shores lie the great industrial centres of Chicago, Detroit, Cleveland and Toronto—has reached an advanced state of pollution which is irreversible by natural processes.

At the request of the two governments a mixed Canadian and American commission has undertaken a study which has gone on for several years on the two worst affected, Lake Erie and Lake Ontario, which are joined to one another by the Niagara river.

Population explosion

From a report based on studies which were pursued between 1964 and 1970 it appears that the population around their shores has multiplied 150 times since the beginning of the 19th century, and that the increase is likely to go on at an accelerated pace in the coming fifty years, so that it will double again by the year 2020.

The rich deposits of minerals, petroleum and natural gas have given rise to tremendous industrial activity, ranging from car factories and steel plants to petrochemical and textile manufactures. The extraction and contamination of water resulting from these affects, therefore, a very dense population and an industrial production which is both important and varied. In Lakes Erie and Ontario 945 million gallons a day are drawn off for drinking and domestic use by the Americans and Canadians who live around their shores. During the same twenty-four hours, partly for industry and partly for thermal and nuclear power stations, 109 thousand million gallons are pumped from the two lakes and are subsequently, for the most part, discharged back into them. All these forms of pollution, from contamination caused by hydrocarbons emanating from refineries or intensive navigation to thermal pollution from nuclear power stations, as well as that from sewage and detergents, continue to increase.

Much of the responsibility can be pinned on the fertilizers used in the basin of Lake Erie for agricultural purposes, which were found to have contained 89,000 tons of phosphorus. 70 per cent of the pollution arises from detergents in urban waste water.

Six of the aquatic recreation centres on Lake Erie have had to be closed down on account of the risks they presented to their users. And the White House has despatched American army engineers to attack pollution on the lake.

Lake Michigan is less affected, but even if one could put a stop im-mediately to all the contamination entering it, 500 years would still elapse before a satisfactory equilibrium could be achieved. Irreversible pollution?

Diseases carried by water, such as viral hepatitis, cholera or typhoid appear or reappear, despite the progress of hygiene. Can we wonder, when we find that the standard figure in Germany, in oxidation tests for measuring the drinkability of water, is 12 milligrammes per litre of permanganate of potassium, and that the figure recorded on the Elbe was 5 mg/l in 1880, 13 in 1910, 30 in 1930, 42 in 1940, 70 in 1950 and 80 in 1960?

Threat to life

Pollution is winning.

Men have wasted and spoiled one of the richest, most agreeable, least costly and most indispensable of their assets.

And today life is threatened; the world is thirsty.

Plan proposed for an enormous underground reserve of water, to supply London from the western parts of the Thames valley

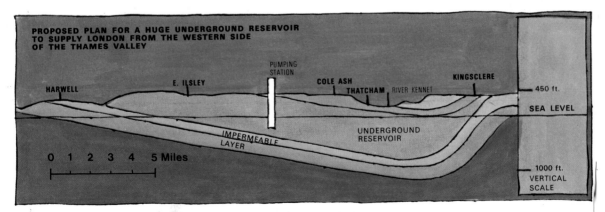

PROPOSED PLAN FOR A HUGE UNDERGROUND RESERVOIR
TO SUPPLY LONDON FROM THE WESTERN SIDE
OF THE THAMES VALLEY

HARWELL   E. ILSLEY   PUMPING STATION   COLE ASH   THATCHAM   RIVER KENNET   KINGSCLERE   450 ft.   SEA LEVEL

IMPERMEABLE LAYER   UNDERGROUND RESERVOIR

0 1 2 3 4 5 Miles

1000 ft. VERTICAL SCALE

CHAPTER 7

THE WORLD'S THIRST

The water which circulates in the land, the rivers, the streams, the oceans and the atmosphere of our planet totals 324 million cubic miles. But, alas, only 3 per cent of this vast quantity of liquid is fresh; more than 97 per cent comprises bitter lakes and salt seas. Moreover, a little more than three-quarters of the fresh water is composed of the polar ice-caps and is therefore inaccessible. All that remains available is the fresh water of lakes, rivers and streams, about 30,300 cubic miles, plus subterranean water amounting to 2,000,000 cubic miles. The figure defies the imagination, which feels drowned at the very thought of it. But nevertheless the world is already thirsty.

Unequal distribution

Steelworks and rolling mills consume considerable quantities of water, and until lately their growth in Lorraine was not called into question, since a vast amount of room was available. The situation is no longer the same. The new works at Sollac had to spend large sums of money when installed in order to obtain the necessary water supplies. At Dunkirk, in the Pas de Calais, the installation of a metallurgical plant became a nightmare when suddenly, after all the plans and calculations had been made, the problem of available water supply arose. More and more iron is imported by France by sea-routes and it has become more economical to install the steelworks in the neighbourhood of ports. With plans drawn up and work put in hand, the necessity of water was suddenly remembered, and it happens to be scarce in this region. Would it have to be brought by digging a 37-mile canal? Would a dam have to be built to form a reservoir? Would the water have to be pumped out of the sea and all the pipework reconstructed or the brine demineralized to enable the original pipes to be used? Eventually it was decided to take a chance on drawing the water from canals and recycling the used water as much as possible in order to reduce the amount pumped out.

There is an abundance of water on the surface of the globe but it is not equally distributed. Sometimes it is salt, sometimes it is absent altogether, sometimes it is badly contaminated. The whole world is thirsty.

Shortage of water overtook the central and Mediterranean areas of Spain and the Côte d'Azur in France about ten years ago. In summer 200,000 people every day at Toulon

Water-carrier at Puente del Arzobispo, in Spain

A small village in
Castille. Chickens
peck in the old
river-bed (left, above)

Vaux de Vire in the
fog—Calvados
(left, below)

Iceberg on the east
coast of Greenland
(above)

Lake Titicaca, in Peru
(right)

Belem. One branch
of the Amazon at its
outlet: it wanders
about among a
thousand islands
which the river keeps
shifting . . .

are deprived of water from six in the evening until dawn. The pinch is beginning to be felt in Britain, Belgium and the Netherlands.

At Tokyo, in 1964, forty-one days of drought disrupted the city supply, and domestic water was cut off during part of the day, being restricted in populated areas to the public fountains, at which the inhabitants had to queue up. In 1965, New York, economic capital of the richest and most powerful country in the world, was overtaken by the same trouble and the washing of cars and the watering of gardens was forbidden. London, whose supply network is widespread, fears that in the next five years it will not be possible to provide enough water for the people of the city and suburbs. Amsterdam, though only slightly affected, is at the mercy of a succession of hot days or a sharp dose of pollution in the Rhine. The Ruhr only survives because of severe legislation, and Paris only because nine-tenths of the population are away during the month of August. Southern California suffers from thirst despite giant projects, as does New York State, which is forbidden by Canada to increase its appropriations from the Great Lakes, and by the Supreme Court of the United States to draw more from the upper course of the Delaware river, for in the lower valley the reservoirs which supply Philadelphia had been heavily tapped and their levels were consequently so low that they were being invaded by sea-water.

Yet the Amazon, below its delta at Belem, thrusts into the ocean a fresh-water current of such size and strength (a fifth of all the fresh water in the world) that it is still perceptible a hundred miles out to sea, and Lake Baikal, in the middle of Siberia, is filled with water so pure that drivers top up the batteries of their cars

. . . while in Rio de
Janeiro, also in
Brazil, people have
to carry water
wearily on their
heads, several gallons
at a time

with it . . . and it represents 18 per cent of the world's reserves of fresh water, also unused. These could not prevent the crisis in Scotland in 1959, when the Spey, whose water gives the local whisky its particular flavour, was drying up. Man has established himself on the banks of the most desirable water-courses and then multiplied. But water has not followed his example; it has not concentrated or increased.

Growing needs

The world has always had need of water, and from Moses to the water-diviners of yesterday and the hydrologists of today its discoverers have been acclaimed. Confrontations, wars, shifts of population and dead towns have from the beginning of time been connected with the discovery or disappearance of water sources. Though the problem is always real and agonizing it presents a variety of aspects. The shortage of a viable water supply can take many forms, all of which represent thirst. At Dakar it is the problem of supply, of insufficient means of distribution, which condemns the population to interminable daily queueing. In the Philippines it is the multiplicity of wells in the coastal area for irrigating the ricefields which has caused the intrusion of sea water; the rice crop there is naturally getting worse and worse. In Israel it is the desert which makes it necessary to supply 98 per cent of dwellings by pipeline, and it is the same desert which has driven Egypt to build the Aswan Dam and which obliges the port of Nouakchott, capital of Mauritania, to transport its water from a well 40 miles away and to build a factory for desalinating sea water. Water abounds at Calcutta, but this does not prevent the drinking water re-

quirements of the 8 million inhabitants from exceeding the capacity of the supply system by 44 million gallons every day. So people quench their thirst with the unfiltered water of the Hooghly river, or draw from the 3,500 wells which have been dug at random in the town. It is thirst too which compels those women in Indonesia or Cameroun to carry a few litres of water in a gourd on their head. And there is this extra risk. The experts of WHO[1] have established that the frequency of

[1] World Health Organization, an agency of the United Nations.

TOTAL URBAN POPULATION HAVING NEED OF NEW SUPPLY NETWORKS OR EXTENSION OF EXISTING NETWORKS BETWEEN NOW AND 1977 IN 75 DEVELOPING COUNTRIES
Population in thousands of inhabitants

Region	Urban population needing new networks or extensions in 1962	Forecast of increase in urban population which will need extension of supply in 1977	Total	Percentage of total in 75 countries
North Africa	4,190	13,720	17,910	5
Africa S. of Sahara	10,150	11,110	21,260	7
Africa, total	14,340	24,830	39,170	12
Central America and W. Indies	4,270	23,440	27,710	8
Tropical S. America	7,150	43,640	50,790	15
Temperate S. America	2,440	9,290	11,730	4
Latin America, total	13,860	76,370	90,230	27
S.W. Asia	6,575	20,720	27,295	8
S. Central Asia	62,570	44,200	106,770	32
S.E. Asia	24,190	29,630	53,820	16
E. Asia	7,120	11,250	18,970	5
Asia, total	100,455	105,800	206,855	61
TOTAL	128,655	207,000	336,255	100

intestinal maladies diminishes by 30 per cent if a family can have access to water near their home instead of having to transport it over long distances.

Water requirements

One can be thirsty on the shore of an ocean, beside a polluted river or a few miles from a spring.

At Bandoeng water is sold in buckets at five times the price it costs in New York. How can water shortage and thirst be avoided? Ghana has calculated that the capital, Accra, will have tripled in population by 1980 and that the daily requirement of water will rise from 20 million gallons to 88 million. How can this growing thirst in a developing country be quenched? A statistical table published by the United Nations indicates the acuteness of this problem (page 104).

One dry phrase in the report, more telling than a diatribe, sums up the thirst of a third of the world: "70 per cent of the urban population of these countries either have an inadequate supply with no mains, or use dangerous water or both. The rate rises to 90 per cent outside the larger towns."

Underdeveloped areas

Thus two worlds live side by side, suffering from shortage of water for opposite reasons. On the one hand thirst results from lack of water in desert areas or from the existence of open water which may be abundant but is undrinkable and unfiltered; on the other hand the problem is water which is overloaded to a degree at which it becomes both undrinkable and unusable.

In the underdeveloped countries it is lack of industrialization which leads to thirst, here it is industrial-

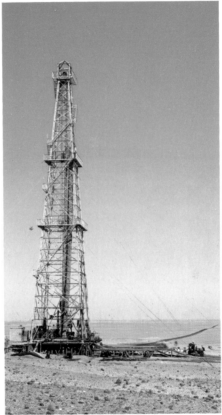

Windmill for pumping water in Brazil

Oil-drilling on the shore of the Red Sea

Inauguration ceremony in Haiti of the irrigation canal built in 1830 and recently brought into use again

One of the largest fresh-water reservoirs in the world: Lake Baikal, in Siberia; in autumn, winter and summer

sure is one of the origins of thirst on both sides of the equator. The growth of large towns in countries which are in process of development is still more rapid than that of towns in the developed countries, important though these are. The cumulative effect of this increased consumption is felt everywhere. It demands a concerted effort. Finally, although a peasant in a rural area of an underdeveloped country now uses 9 gallons of water a day and an American citizen 1,300 gallons, representing agricultural and industrial requirements, both are increasing their consumption regularly and relentlessly, which brings us back to our original situation vis-à-vis a mass of water which has not altered over thousands of years. In order to quench the universal thirst, a combined global effort is needed. If present trends continue, and everything indicates that they will, the consumption of water will escalate considerably, for its users will have doubled once more in 60 years—4,000 million in 1980. And perhaps 8,000 million by 2000. Will there then be enough water?

Ever-rising consumption

Over and above the increase in the number of thirsty consumers there is, as we have seen, the increase in daily demand which accrues as the standard of life improves.

Thus consumption in France, for metal industries, electricity and various manufacturing plants, irrigation and drinking water, has risen from 22 thousand million cubic yards in 1960 to 42 thousand million in 1970—almost double in ten years.

The American estimates for 1954, 1980 and 2000 are also eloquent. Water used for cooling electrical generating plant will increase from

ization which is causing it. There it is failure to harness water which impedes agriculture; here it is the intensive use of water in agriculture which absorbs too much of it and at the same time pollutes it.

But thirst is rampant everywhere, whether chronic or acute, latent or anticipated.

Some common factors link both worlds and produce, willy-nilly, a state of solidarity between them. In the first place they both occupy the same planet, which is one and indivisible, in which any project, particularly if concerned with the manipulation of the hydrological cycle in the world, must itself be one and indivisible.

Furthermore, demographic pres-

62 thousand million gallons per day in 1954 to 358 thousand million in 1980; for industry in general from 28 thousand million to 192 thousand million; for irrigation from 147·0 thousand million to 147·2 thousand million; and for town supply from 16 thousand million to 35 thousand million. A total increase from 253 thousand million gallons every twenty-four hours to 732 thousand million.

This is for the United States alone, with an estimated population for the year 2000 of 300 million, as compared with 4,000 million for the whole of the globe.

Against this universal multiplication of man and his needs can be set the two considerable totals of the

fresh water in circulation, polluted or not, produced by calculations for the whole planet — 30,300 cubic miles for surface waters and 2,000,000 cubic miles for subterranean waters.

In reality this does not amount to very much, firstly because the whole of this colossal mass is not at our disposal. It is not conceivable, for example, that we should hope to exploit subterranean reserves to the last drop when sometimes they have taken centuries to accumulate. Interference with more than 10 per cent of these hidden waters poses the danger of creating disequilibrium so that the use of more than 200,000 cubic miles could not be envisaged. Similarly we cannot hope to have at our disposal the whole of the surface waters, both because all are not accessible or obtainable and because pollution limits or will limit their use, even supposing that they would be recycled. In the end this leaves only a little more than 4,800 cubic miles a year for the human race.

Basing our calculations on the rate of consumption which will have been achieved in the United States between now and then — 1,950 cubic yards per year per American, and setting this figure against the 15 thousand million population forecast by demographers for the year 2030 . . . after the end of that year not one extra human being will be able to be supported unless something is done about the situation now.

Those who foretell the future assert that unless vigorous communal action is taken on a global scale, catastrophes will be widespread after 2010, and by 2050 man will have been wiped out on Earth.

As the world's population increases, so does the number of dams. Left: two stages in the building of the Aswan Dam, inaugurated in January, 1971, after ten years' work

Brasilia could not have been built in the heart of Brazil if a dam had not supplied it with water and power

Brasilia — the new capital of Brazil

*Sunshine, clean water, healthy plants,
and the result —satisfactory test-fish*

CHAPTER 8

ORGANIZING PURITY

We utilize water; we do not consume it. What we consume is its purity.

The global mass of water is always identical in itself, but here it flows copiously, there it is far away or even non-existent, elsewhere it is contaminated. Water, constant but at the same time fickle, follows its own rules and resists coercion. And it uses all manner of means for imposing respect. Today man is paying dearly for having forgotten this, and if he still wants to rely on water tomorrow he can only do so by ceasing to abuse it. Water is amiable, genial and understanding, and will offer itself willingly if man, in re-creating the environment which he has so shamelessly altered, learns how to shape it so as to restore to water all the consideration owed to its overriding importance.

Task of Hercules

The resources must be husbanded and augmented by management and exploration; the programme can be formulated in a few words, but it covers a multitude of activities, hundreds of decisions, thousands of studies and projects by the million. Supplying drinking water to the men, women and children of five continents already resembles one of the tasks of Hercules. Providing water in sufficient quantity and of satis-factory quality presents problems wherever human life exists. At Calcutta or Dakar, certainly, but also in Los Angeles and London.

Assuming that sufficient water is available, supplying one French family of five persons with pure running water costs approximately 2,000 dollars (the French franc is approximately worth 18 cents), which can be broken down into 450 dollars for the mains and distribution network, 100 dollars for conditioning and 1,450 dollars for installations in and around the actual dwelling. But if the water has to be brought a long way, or if the population grows to such an extent that there is a scarcity, the cost rises considerably. Thus Los Angeles, in California, has to look for water hundreds of miles away. Anyway, California is becoming a gigantic hydraulic complex of canals, dams and pumping stations which collect, store and then distribute all the usable water from Arizona to Oregon. 80 per cent of the Americans in California live in the southern two-thirds of the state, which receives less than a quarter of the rainfall, and most of the rain comes in winter, while Californian agriculture is crying out for water in summer. Today half the water employed in California emanates from rivers and streams fed by canals and aqueducts which are

themselves supplied by hundreds of storage reservoirs. Tomorrow San Francisco and Los Angeles will be supplied with water originating from the region of Sacramento, stored by dams, pumped at various stations and transported by aqueducts. The water from a tap in San Francisco will have run a course of more than 500 miles, and the Los Angeles aqueduct is 140 miles long.

What will be the cost price of a gallon of pure water at San Francisco or Los Angeles?

The size of installations and works reach the same gigantic proportions in the basin of the Colorado, which is to south-west America what the Nile is to Egypt, as do those for the harnessing of the Delaware which supplies New York, and whose water is the subject of dispute between that city and Philadelphia. There are 21 dams and 52 waterworks. For the business of obtaining pure water is becoming more and more dependent upon the elimination of waste. The aqueduct which brings water from the Delaware to New York will be able to supply the deficiencies of the Hudson.

On the continents liable to famine, Asia, Africa and Latin America, the works to be carried out are less complex, but the need is just as

The scientific use of water, without pollution, has brought excellent crops to a once-dreary landscape. Building of a dam in the Sertao, Brazil: (1) the countryside; (2) mines laid in rows; (3) last drilling; (4) water turned on; (5) a field of maize

urgent and as onerous. The findings of the United Nations are set out in a table on page 114.

In short—6 thousand million dollars for providing a third of the world with wholesome water for domestic use.

Natural pesticides

Good management involves foresight and planning.

And this means forestalling the indiscriminate and needless accumulation in sources of water of toxic substances which do more harm than good. The United States provides an example. There the farmers

Region	Urban population which will need new services or extensions in 1977, in thousands of inhabitants	Installation costs	
		In thousands of U.S. dollars	Annual mean in percentage of PNB of 1960

WATER REQUIREMENTS OF TOWNS AND COST OF INSTALLATION
(Not including work for improving existing systems or the quality, quantity and pressure.)

Region	Urban population which will need new services or extensions in 1977, in thousands of inhabitants	In thousands of U.S. dollars	Annual mean in percentage of PNB of 1960
North Africa	17,910	447,100	0·31
Africa S. of Sahara	21,260	474,500	0·22
Africa, total	39,170	921,600	0·25
Central America and W. Indies	27,710	668,500	0·26
Tropical S. America	50,790	1,162,800	0·29
Temperate S. America	11,730	244,900	0·11
Latin America, total	90,230	2,076,200	0·24
S.W. Asia	27,295	408,400	0·17
S. Central Asia	106,770	1,338,900	0·20
S.E. Asia	53,820	806,900	0·30
E. Asia	18,970	284,300	0·61
Asia, total	206,855	2,838,500	0·23
TOTAL	336,255	5,836,300	0·24

are using ever fewer pesticides, especially organo-chlorides of which DDT is a type, for destroying harmful insects. To protect their crops of corn or fruit they obtain a yearly supply of eggs of the praying mantis or of microscopic wasps. *Tricho-* *gramma* wasps, a quarter the size of a pin's head, work wonders, and together with the mantis they decimate the lice, greenfly and other scourges of modern agriculture.

In the U.S.S.R. another method is employed which also avoids the

These oil-pumping plants on the Red Sea shore mean that Egypt gets the petrol it requires

use of pesticides. Swarms of males of a harmful species are exposed to X-rays or other forms of electromagnetic radiation. Thus sterilized, they are liberated among the crops which it is desired to protect. They mate in vain with the local females . . . and no water is polluted.

The day will arrive, certainly in the near future, when, following all these traumatic experiences with pesticides and detergents, laws will prescribe that every new product must be tested as to its effects upon water before it can be allowed to come on to the market.

Foresight. . . . It is to cure hunger and prevent famine that so many developing countries construct irrigation networks. In this way they increase their crops. But in their haste to see water flowing in their fields they omit to weigh the consequences. In the Congo they drew from a "tributary" of Lake Tanganyika the water which enabled tens of thousands of farms to be established. It was contaminated by bilharzia. The whole population is now affected and debilitated by the infection, while another stream, only 450 yards away, free from infestation, offered an alternativ

for little extra effort. And this is not an isolated case. In the Sudan, the United Arab Republic, Rhodesia, Morocco, and every place where the irrigation canals do not flow swiftly enough to prevent the snail which carries bilharziosis from breeding (a situation which obviously costs a lot to rectify), bilharzia spreads. Is it worthwhile to win proteins by creating invalids?

Clean water is an asset, and like all assets it pays for itself.

Revitalizing water

Without purification good management is impossible. One cannot administer cubic miles of mud, algae, effluents or organic compounds; one cannot manage unhealthy streams or contaminated rivers. One suffers them. All the means exist for clarifying, purifying and revitalizing any water without exception. Either by skimming, decantation, biologically, by bacterial bed or activated sludge, by anaerobic digestion, flocculation, slow or rapid filtration, chlorination or "true" ozonization, every type of degraded water can be made to regain its vitality. "True" ozoniza-

The growth of towns means new purification plants. Here is one at Mont-Valérien, near Paris

Manual work, using old methods . . .

tion, for example, by recharging the water with oxygen, can guarantee a cure in all cases of contamination by detergents, phenols or hydrocarbons, the most detestable of pollutants. In the laboratory ozone has even proved effective against carcinogenic hydrocarbons and certain organo-chloride pesticides.

Man possesses the means of cleaning all dirty water.

But water purification is costly; it is easier and less annoying, if one dislikes the skin of boiled milk, to filter it off when pouring it into the coffee rather than to fish it out bit by bit . . . and less expensive than to throw out the contents through sheer laziness and make another cup. The Ruhr region has come to understand this. Its complex organization, which brings together 250

municipalities and 2,200 industrial enterprises in one co-operative, is governed by two rules: everyone pays in proportion to the pollution which he causes (thus all have an interest in keeping contamination at bay), and the payments are used to purify the water and organize their management.

The Orsanco in the valley of the Ohio, which traverses one of the richest regions of the United States, has constituted around the 1,000 miles of the river and its tributaries a governing body with its headquarters at Cincinnati. Every hour automatic electronic measuring apparatus sends information to the centre as to the oxygen content of the water and such items as conductivity and temperature. Every departure from normal is followed up by enquiry and action. The waterworks complete the diagnosis by chemical and bacteriological analysis before treatment is decided upon. This important piece of good management only costs, we are told, 200 dollars per mile per year for the 11·5 million inhabitants of this oasis of purity. This even surpasses the Ruhr.

The extreme remedy, obviously, would be to close all possible avenues of pollution. But pesticides render valuable service and combat hunger, hydrocarbons fuel thousands of motors, and detergents clean so many articles and clothes that the already industrialized world cannot put the clock back. The Soviet government recently decided to close a cellulose factory set up on the shores of Lake Baikal, which had

. . . gives way to complex, automated plants

begun to pillage the 45 million years' old waters which harbour several hundred species of animal life not found elsewhere in the world, and which represent 80 per cent of the Soviet reserves of fresh water. This courageous decision claims respect for its intelligence and sets an example for all the virgin territories of the world. But for the Thames or Seine valleys, the area around Milan or the great American lakes, it is too late to close the factories and plants, the mines and the boreholes; cleaning up operations must be carried out to improve conditions.

Water itself is not used up; it is its qualities which are consumed. The solution, then, is to form towns, basins, regions, even nations, into integrated associations in which projects are complementary rather than competitive, and in which recycling is practised to regenerate exhausted or overloaded water in such a way that the smallest drop is utilized over and over again. Thus, if its usage is well balanced, a river can serve four purposes. In the face of increased pollution, continuous treatment after successive utilizations can restore water to a condition which allows constant use. This involves the reproduction by men, at will and on a small scale, of the hydrological cycle which carries drops from ocean to ocean via clouds, rain, percolation, springs, rivers and streams, and which constantly revitalizes water.

Systems of this type exist in a few towns, at Bielefeld, in Germany, for example. They will eventually become commonplace. In the near future they will integrate factories which are fed by their clean circuit and associations will be formed; this has already been suggested in the U.S.A. At Windhoek, in South-West Africa, the water from the town's sluices is turned into drinking

water. Technically anything is possible.

This will avoid regrettable incidents such as happened in France —the disappearance of 19 miles of a river.

Global survey

But this will not be enough. The double pressure of population increase and growing demand presupposes extra supplies of water. And in the first place a knowledge of the resources available for reasonable use will have to be the basis of both local and global administra-tion of water supplies. A global survey would lead to the satisfactory solution of local problems.

This was behind the reasoning of UNESCO in 1965 when all the nations of the world were invited to take part in the "International Hydrological Decade", which will end, of course, in 1975. The objects are as follows: to undertake a detailed physical study of the hydro-logical cycle—precipitation, eva-poration, surface flow and seepage —which will provide fundamental information for a searching analysis of the general cycle and will allow an accurate assessment of manage-

The dam at Bratsk, in Siberia

The living water of the mountains, part of the "unharnessed energy" in the cycle of water, means there are still unused supplies (left, above)

Water-cannon, used in Siberia to clear away earth (left, below)

119

ment possibilities. A world balance sheet will be drawn up.

On one side will appear the total of resources together with their locality and the rational means of using them. On the other side will be listed the old mistakes due to ignorance, which will now be more easy to avoid, like dams which are too vast, too costly and never used to capacity, or misapplied pumping operations for irrigation which have denuded the soil of its subterranean water. The loss of this underground water has opened up crevasses in Arizona big enough to hold a motor car, and split the earth over 12 or 20 miles, necessitating the abandonment of thousands of acres of fertile land, caused some houses in San Diego, California, to subside one storey, and compelled the layout of the irrigation system to be changed three times every year.

Today the study of Lake Chad for the purpose of utilizing its water, for which infra-red rays, aircraft and satellites have been mobilized to measure evaporation, is more advanced than the study of the River Danube.

Modern dams

Whichever way one turns the notion of unity persists—integrated associations for purifying and revitalizing water, communal studies to discover the best methods of utilization, and, of course, complex and balanced confederations for the collection and employment of water.

The Tennessee valley was the first example of this type. The organization set up, called the TVA (Tennessee Valley Authority), undertook the exploitation of the Wilson Dam on the Tennessee river in Alabama. Four other dams were successively acquired and a further 21 constructed. As a result the Tennessee

became navigable over 600 miles, electricity was supplied to an area of 98,000 square miles and new pastures were created by the TVA. The population increased by more than a million, and revenue rose from 45 per cent of the American average to nearly 80 per cent.

The Bratsk Dam on the Angara, the only river flowing out of Lake Baikal, plays the same rôle in Central Siberia as the TVA in America. Towns and 40 factories have arisen on the great icy wastes. Bratsk, a town of 100,000 inhabitants, did not even exist a few years ago.

The Aswan Dam, in Egypt, has allowed 2·5 million acres of cultivatable land to be won from the desert, and the town which sprang up between the Temples of Philae and Abu Simbel in the wake of the tourist trade has already set up a fertilizer factory, model farms and sugar refineries.

Similar schemes are projected on the Senegal, the Rio de la Plata, the Volta in Ghana, the Damodar in India, and the Mekong in the Indo-Chinese peninsula, where one of the greatest reservoirs in the world would be created on the frontier between the countries of Thailand and Laos.

In every case several nations have an interest in the same project, for the size of these schemes, allied to their necessity, compels men to collaborate. In this category is the AWAPA project, in which Canada, the United States and Mexico are jointly concerned and whose implementation by the Ralph M. Parsons Corporation will require ten years of planning and will cost 100,000 million dollars.

At the same time Soviet Russia has formulated her plan for the period up to the year 2000, for re-establishing the hydrologic balance

of the Caspian Sea, in which the water level is falling and the sturgeon are providing less and less caviare for Iran and Moscow, and also for removing the danger of a shortage of water in her south European industrial and agricultural regions. The scheme involves damming the Petchora and diverting 10 cubic miles per annum to the Volga, transferring water from the Ob in Siberia to Central Asia and Kazakhstan, diverting the north European rivers Vytchegda, Souklona and Onega to the Volga, Don and Dnieper, and creating a gigantic fluvial artery uniting the great rivers of Siberia.

More modestly, but just as efficiently, the Loire basin will be organized in the years to come. 1,630,000 acres could become irrigatable, and anti-pollution treatment would be accompanied by increased capacity for the production of electricity.

Individually and collectively, men

are learning how to utilize water.

But all this will not be enough, because of the population explosion and the increase in demand, both personal and for industry and agriculture. Management is not just research, distribution and organization, it is all of these co-ordinated in pursuance of the principle of economy.

Enormous quantities of water are frittered away without benefit. This happens in irrigation, where far too much water is used—6,000 cubic yards per acre in a season, when 3,000 would suffice if a sprinkling process were employed. Technical modifications of this type would allow the area of irrigation to be doubled everywhere. Why wait? In the south of France, for example, the canals are so primitive that with the amount of water now used 495,000 acres could be watered in place of the 126,000 now covered. Evaporation, too, aggravates the wastage, especially in open reser-

voirs. In the Colorado basin the amount of water lost in this way every year equals the amount used in irrigation. On the other side of the world 40 per cent of the White Nile escapes to the sky in the same way. To build up huge works, dam rivers and store reserves only to see 40 per cent of the treasure lost is an ill-rewarded effort. In the laboratory, with the aid of monomolecular films, it has been possible to reduce evaporation by 70 per cent. In the field two large-scale experiments are in progress, one in the United States, the other in South Africa.

Losses by percolation in irrigation are another source of wastage. Every drop of water is too precious to allow up to 20 per cent of its total volume to seep away without profit on its way to the fields, often causing damage into the bargain. Percolation can lead to a rise in the level of the underground water-table, followed by saturation of the soil, generally accompanied by an

Tamed landscapes. The oasis of El Golea in the Sahara; left, the artificial sea of the Ob, in Siberia; and above, Cambodia

123

increase in salinity and a reduction in crops. This has happened with the Indus. Trials have been carried out with moulded slabs of concrete and with concrete projections over the canals. The benefits from this method are both real and lasting. But this expedient places a burden on investment, although the longevity of the concrete repays the expense of installation in the long run, so that in the end it emerges as the cheapest course of action.

A practical demonstration has been made in the Argentine, in the province of San Juan, on the irrigation network at Caucete. Rendering the canals impermeable over an area of 18,150 acres has allowed the irrigation of an extra 2,220 acres by cutting down seepage. And calculations made by the water department of the Argentine government show benefits which amount to six times the cost of the work.

Other methods have been tried, such as asphalt and covering with bituminous canvas or sheets of plastic, the lasting qualities of which are not yet known. Satisfactory experiments have also been carried out in the Sudan and in Pakistan. But why only there; why wait everywhere else?

Water losses

There is much preoccupation, and rightly so, with these losses of water, but there should be no less enthusiasm about the collection of precipitation. 4,000 years ago farmers in Israel used to collect and accumulate rain water by means of trenches dug in the undulations of the hills, and although the rainfall was never more than 4 inches per annum they managed to cultivate soil which today lies barren. In the Colorado basin, where the water supply is insufficient, the amount extracted from the river when stored only amounts to 10 per cent of the precipitation. Once again, why wait?

Where are extra resources of fresh water to be found? Underground. They are lying dormant 2,600 feet below the surface, in the upper layer of the earth's crust: 2 million cubic miles of water, 3,000 times the amount of water carried at any given moment by the whole of the world's water-courses, which would take 130 years to fill these reservoirs under the ground.

In Iran, 3,000 years ago, men cut subterranean canals, invisible from above, which brought water to the surface by gravitation, sometimes over a distance of many miles. Nobody has counted them, but their number has been estimated at 30,000, and they irrigate half the arable land of the country.

Their value to us is incalculable. Firstly, because 60 per cent of underdeveloped countries on this planet are arid or semi-arid and could be exploited if their subsoil proved to be well-endowed with hidden water, and secondly, because these buried reservoirs could serve as a balance or regulator in regions where the total precipitation, though in itself adequate, is unequally distributed between the seasons, a situation which obtains in all monsoon countries.

This remote source has not been entirely neglected up to now, and the north of France, like industrial Britain, the Ruhr steel region, agricultural California and the developed area around Milan have made large withdrawals from this free reserve. Turkmenistan, in the U.S.S.R., an important industrial region with oil-wells, industries, railways and ports, could hardly exist were it not for water extracted from the subsoil.

But, in general, pumping for

factories or irrigation works has only been carried out haphazardly and at a shallow depth. It is now a question of digging more deeply and working in a more scientific manner so as not to repeat today the errors of yesterday. If the underground reservoirs are emptied the ground subsides or streams disappear.

In the Libyan desert, with the help of the FAO, the United Arab Republic has brought several million acres into use; thanks to an underground reservoir, Saudi Arabia is taking the same road. Geologists of the FAO have also earmarked subterranean reserves in Chad, Salvador, Greece, Haiti, Israel, Syria and Turkey . . . reserves generally of sufficient importance to irrigate between 75,000 and 250,000 acres of barren and lifeless land.

Subterranean water is part of what has been called by science our "natural resources", a category which also includes minerals, soils, forests, sources of energy, fossil deposits, etc.

The Resources and Transport division of the United Nations, often mandated and supported by the UNDP (United Nations Development Programme) is displaying activity in the sphere of underground water which deserves attention.

In Africa the Resources and Transport division, by means of geophysical prospecting (electric and seismic), has made satisfactory and promising soundings in Upper Volta

In the future it is hoped that it will no longer be necessary to test water

and Togoland, and has carried out research in Senegal along the granite belt which stretches across the continent as far as Uganda and suffers particularly in the dry season. Water exists there everywhere in isolated pockets. In Madagascar artesian water has been brought to light—a yield of 15 gallons per second in the barren coastal plain in the west, which can now be irrigated.

In Latin America the region of Mendoza (Argentina), which possesses a rich wine-growing soil but suffers from water shortage, has been explored. Subterranean water exists; it has been found. But before tapping the reservoirs the Resources and Transport division has set up an analogue model which allows the fluctuations of subterranean water resulting from pumping and natural replenishment to be fore-

seen, since the region gets no practical benefit from precipitation. Thus future users do not run the risk of finding, after ill-judged pumping operations, that the ground becomes uncultivatable. In the months to come Togoland will benefit from the same procedure.

Cyprus and the Lebanon, in the Middle East, will soon be provided with hydrological charts of subterranean waters (supplies in the Lebanon are pronounced "fantastic" by the experts) with indications of potential resources of water under the earth, possible yield per square mile, quality of water, drillings and springs.

On the frontier between Pakistan and Afghanistan, in the desert of Tar, in Asia, at Madras for supplying the town with subterranean water . . . briefly the Resources and Transport division has under way 18 projects for extraction of subterranean water in 17 countries of

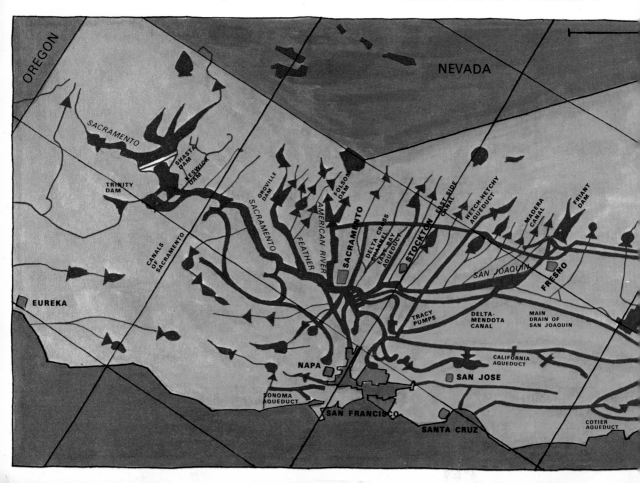

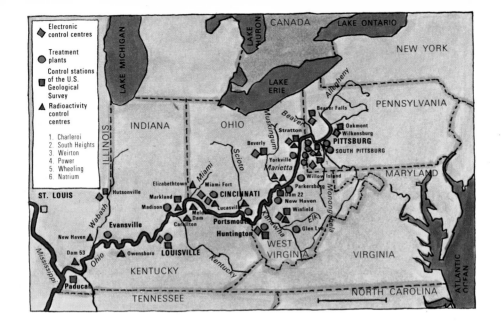

the third world (Dahomey, Honduras, Mali, Mauritania, Peru, etc.).

It is on enterprises such as these that man's hope of sufficient water in the future rests; and it behoves us all to face up to the alarming possibility of the world's thirst leading to widespread death and disaster, and thus to support every means of economy and harnessing of available resources.

(Reference. Picture taken from *Rendez-vous 1980* by the same author. Editions Cayot, Paris. Copyright UNO.)

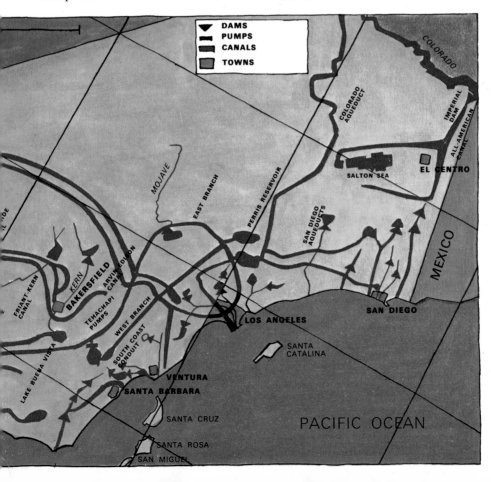

INDEX

BIBLIOGRAPHY

Bardach, John, 1964. *Downstream: A Natural History of the River.* Harper & Row (U.S.)
Brittain, Robert, 1958. *Rivers, Man and Myths.* Longmans.
Davis, Kenneth S., 1953. *River on the Rampage.* Doubleday (U.S.).
Davis, Kenneth S., and John Arthur Day, 1964. *Water, The Mirror of Science.* Heinemann Educ.
Fisher, J. 1970. *The Wonderful World of the Sea.* Macdonald.
Gal, P., 1970. *From a Raindrop to the Ocean.* Sadler.
King, Thomson, 1961. *Water Miracle of Nature.* Collier-Macmillan (U.S.)
Langbein, Walter B. and William G. Hoyt, 1959. *Water Facts for the Nation's Future.* Ronald Press (U.S.)
Leopold, Luna B., and Walter B. Langbein, 1960. *A Primer on Water.* U.S. Government Printing Office (U.S.).
Rossotti, H. 1970. *H₂O.* Oxford University Press.
Walton, W. C. 1970. *The World of Water.* Weidenfeld & Nicolson.
Water, 1970. Macdonald Educational.
Water, 1970. Time-Life (U.K. and U.S.).